When a Mate Wants Out

SALLY CONWAY

JIM CONWAY

ZondervanPublishingHouse

Grand Rapids, Michigan

A Division of HarperCollinsPublishers

When a Mate Wants Out
Copyright © 1992 by Sally and Jim Conway

Published by Zondervan Publishing House
Grand Rapids, Michigan 49530

Library of Congress Cataloging-in-Publication Data

Conway, Sally.
    When a mate wants out / by Sally Conway, Jim Conway.
      p. cm.
    Includes bibliographical references.
    ISBN 0-310-23647-9
    1. Marriage—United States. 2. Communication in marriage—United
States. 3. Marriage—Religious aspects—Christianity.   I. Conway, Jim.
II. Title.
HQ734.C77   1992
646.7'8—dc20   92-8295
                                               CIP

Edited by Julie Ackerman Link
Designed by Blue Water Ink
Cover design by the Puckett Group

Printed in the United States of America

92 93 94 95 / DH / 5 4 3 2 1

To

John and Jacque Coulombe   Dennis and Karen Dirks

Our support group friends
who have been our
stretcher-bearers
during
Jim's recovery from his dysfunctional family,
Sally's breast cancer,
and the writing of this book.

When a Mate Wants Out

Contents

Introduction

• • •

SINCE 1958, the two of us have spent a great deal of our energy helping people rebuild their crumbling marriages. We did it first while pastoring three different churches. Then in 1981 we formed an organization (Christian Living Resources, Inc./Mid-Life Dimensions) to help couples put their marriages back together.

Through the years many couples close to breaking up came to "Pastor Jim" for help. Since our first books were published at the end of the seventies, we both have been in touch with hundreds of thousands of hurting couples across the nation and in other countries. Of these couples, many have been success stories. So we can say with assurance: *there's hope for your marriage!*

Not everyone succeeds in rebuilding their marriage, but many do. Even the ones whose marriages finally end in divorce tell us they are glad they worked at restoration as long as they did. Instead of having regrets for giving up too soon—as many divorced people later have—they feel satisfied that they tried long and hard to save their marriage. In the process, they grew and became more complete individuals who were better prepared to live as healthy singles.

Not only have we helped others work on their marriages, we have had to work on *our own marriage*. The two of us have had some rough, scary times. Much of what we share with you, we have learned through our own thirty-eight years of marriage. Yes, we've read a lot of books and guided others in putting their marriages back together, but we know firsthand which ideas work. And we're happy to pass them on to you.

Part 1

AT FIRST . . .

Chapter • 1

Don't Panic

• • •

CHERYL WATCHED as Ron jammed some of his clothes into a bag and stuffed his deodorant, hair dryer, and shaver in with them. He wouldn't look at Cheryl. Her eyes saw his every move, but she couldn't get her mouth to say a word. She had run out of things to say. All her pleading had proven useless, and now an awkward stillness hung in the air. Although she was outwardly quiet, a million clamoring noises were pounding inside.[*]

He's leaving! she thought. *Going—I don't know where. He's taking the older car and leaving the better one for the kids and me. It looks as if he's planning to leave forever.*

Ron had been warning Cheryl for weeks that he was going to leave, but she never took his threats seriously. Even though they argued a lot and there was tension between them, she always believed they could work out their problems. But now he was actually leaving! She was devastated.

---

[*] In this story and throughout the book, we are using real people to illustrate real life. In most cases, however, we have changed names and disguised circumstances to protect the privacy of the people involved.

A Common Problem

Unlike many women, Cheryl actually saw her spouse drive away. Many unsuspecting wives come home to find their husbands have moved out without so much as a bitter good-bye. Other husbands, instead of leaving physically, vacate emotionally. They become overly involved with their work, the guys, or another woman in an effort to *escondiendo*—shed themselves of their marriage relationship.

Women do it, too. Larry finally woke up when Joan demanded, "Just get out! I need some space." Larry would have seen the signs along the way if he'd been paying attention, but he was so wrapped up in his career that he had taken Joan and their marriage for granted.

Joan had been happy to mother their three children and keep up with all their activities while they were growing up, but when they became teenagers they were seldom home. Larry didn't realize how alone Joan felt now that the kids no longer needed her as much.

When the new associate pastor asked Joan to be his part-time assistant, Larry thought the experience would be good for her. He was unaware, however, of how many evenings she worked because he himself worked late nearly every night.

Larry also was unaware that Joan's boss made her feel like a new woman. He always complimented her on the work she did and took time to talk to her; in fact, he really seemed to understand her inner feelings. He sensed her loneliness and lack of fulfillment, so he encouraged her to take some college courses and consider a career of her own. Joan liked having a cheerleader.

Before long, Joan and the associate pastor were enjoying each other more than was appropriate. Larry should have sensed that something was wrong when Joan turned colder and colder toward him—but he didn't.

Then Joan announced she was going back to school. This didn't set well with Larry, and he wouldn't hear of it. "You've got enough to do around here without trotting off to college," he argued.

That did it for Joan. With hands on her hips, she yelled, "You're smothering me! It's time for you to get out!"

So What Are You Going to Do Now?

Whether you are a Cheryl whose husband is leaving or a Larry whose wife wants you out of the house, you are in a crisis situation. And whether your spouse is having an affair, threatening to leave, or has already left, beware of how you respond. Actions that are most natural in this type of situation usually make matters worse instead of better.

In the first hours and days after learning that your mate is leaving, you will be in a state of shock, and people have been known to do very foolish things during this critical period.

You may be tempted to shout and stomp and make unreasonable demands. You might feel like crying for hours on end or going on a shopping spree or drinking binge. Maybe you're a quiet tooth-grinder who vows to get revenge. Or perhaps you're the kind of person who withdraws into a shell, fooling yourself into believing that you don't care.

When the Unbelievable Is True

We know about these reactions because we ourselves have faced devastating crises and have often been surprised at how we behaved under stress—sometimes good; sometimes bad.

From those we have counseled over the years, we've learned how shattered they felt when they first learned their mate wanted out. Some of these people have expressed themselves very poignantly, such as in this letter: *distressing to the feelings*

> Please help me! I'm devastated. My husband tells me he doesn't love me like a wife anymore. . . . He has moved out. My pastor, friends, and family all tell me that he's preparing me for divorce, but he says he just wants time to himself to figure out who he is.

Yet he has a friendship with a woman that I find questionable. He is attending public functions with her but denies that anything is going on. The whole thing is driving me nuts. . . .

I love him, but he says he doesn't love me. I'm so confused. I'm ready to throw in the towel, but I really do love him and miss him so much. We've had a far from perfect marriage—but where is my husband? Please, if there is anything you can do, please help me.

Tom's story carries a similar theme of hurt. He and Dorrie had been married fewer than five years when she announced that she wanted a divorce. She despised him and wanted him out of the house *right now!*

She expected to get custody of their little girl, Amy, and was planning to take a promotion out of state. This meant Tom would have little time with their daughter. As all of these facts hit Tom, he thought he would die! He loved Dorrie very much and couldn't believe that her earlier wild passion for him had turned to such a cold, calculating hatred. And he dearly loved Amy. He had been home with her certain days of every week, and the extra hours of parenting had caused his heart to be deeply entwined with her life. It was unbearable to think of seeing her only once or twice a year for a few days!

Tom moved in with a bachelor friend and lived for the times Dorrie would let him care for Amy. Dorrie usually arranged for a third party to deliver Amy so she wouldn't have to face Tom.

Each new phase of the divorce proceedings smashed Tom into yet smaller pieces. But whenever Dorrie spoke civilly to him over the phone, Tom felt as if a few of the fragments had been glued together again. *Maybe this means she is changing her mind and won't go through with the divorce,* he dared to hope. But then she would strike another blow to his already fragmented life.

The anguish and uncertainty was about to kill Tom. He walked around in a daze and became so emotionally upset he had to see a psychiatrist.

This situation doesn't yet have a happy ending, but it shows that men as well as women suffer severe trauma when their marriages are threatened. There are, however, some differences in the way men and women respond to the suffering.

In our years of counseling we have found that men usually reach out for help only once or twice. If the marriage doesn't come together, they quit trying. Most women, though, are willing to work longer to rebuild a broken marriage.

According to several researchers, it is also true that men are more apt to hide their emotions than women. One report says that men, when their marriages start to come undone, tend to withdraw and become silent and secretive. Women, on the other hand, are more inclined to become exceptionally active.[1]

Panic Causes More Panic

At the first threat of separation, some people rush right out and start divorce proceedings. Others talk to everyone they know about what is going on, spreading the information under the guise of a "prayer request." Others dump out all the garbage they have collected about their mate. When a third party is involved, a few have even gone out and bought a gun to take care of the person! Others have wished they had the nerve. None of these solve anything, of course.

The first thing to tell yourself is, *Don't panic*. The truth is, you need to calm yourself and take a good look at the situation. Be still, and don't do anything rash. You probably won't feel like saying "God loves me and has a wonderful plan for my life" while your marriage is crumbling, but be assured that he does have some principles to guide you through this difficult period.

We know you hurt—a lot! You may even wonder if you can live through the awful, gnawing pain. We understand your problem and want to help you. Over the years, we have learned some specific methods to help people restore broken or breaking marriages, and we have discovered that the actions taken at the very beginning of the crisis can make the difference in whether or not a marriage ever comes back together.

The people who usually have the most success in saving their marriages are those who keep their panic under control. Most are not naturally serene people, but they develop a surprising degree of composure and find strength they didn't know they had.

You Are Normal

Don't be discouraged if you're not a super being who is able to handle any mess. The truth is, you *won't* handle everything correctly. No one ever does. We each have our own ways of managing stress, but none of us can save a broken marriage solely with our own wits and winsomeness. It will take God's power working in you and in your mate who's scrambling in the opposite direction.

Since you can't, with your own power, restrain your panic indefinitely—in spite of your best resolves—you will need the inner strength and wisdom that only God can give you. So ask him to control your emotions and perceptions as well as your circumstances.

When a mate leaves, or threatens to do so, there are two things you must do immediately:

Make a conscious decision to *be calm.*

Ask God to *make you calm.*

Thousands who have been in this predicament have been amazed at the courage and strength they received from God. Many have said words to this effect: "If you had asked me a few years ago if I could ever go through such a thing, I would have said that I simply would collapse. Instead, when it actually happened, I was surprised that I had the moment-by-moment ability to endure."

Patty found this to be true. She wrote and told us the sad story of how her husband left, without warning, and went to live with another woman. Then she added:

I keep busy. I go to ballroom dancing with a large group

of people. I go to school three nights a week after work. I go to movies with my girlfriends. I do crafts at home when I have time.

My children are proud of me. Friends at church have said how much I've grown and how great I am doing. My counselor tells me that all through this she has been pleased with how well I am doing.

As I have told them, the only way I'm getting through this, with my sanity, is because God has been with me all the way. I know he really does come to me in direct proportion to my needs. . . .

Once you stop the panic and feel quieter inside, you will be more able to believe that your marriage has a chance. God's peace is in itself a great power-booster and will give you hope.

Chapter • 2

Have Hope

• • •

HOPE DOES NOT DISAPPOINT.... *Hope does not disappoint.... Hope does not disappoint....*[1] This verse has been going around in our heads ever since we began work on this chapter.

HOPE is a foundation stone for success in restoring your marriage. This belief comes from our own experiences and from those of people we've walked alongside during the marital rebuilding process.

Hope keeps the fires burning and the wheels turning. Without hope, plans and aspirations crumble and collapse. You simply won't make it through the inevitable hardships of rebuilding your marriage if you have no *hope* that it can happen.

Hope in the Face of Impossible Odds

Shirley paced the braided rug on the hardwood floor of her country-decorated bedroom. She couldn't bring herself to fluff the bedding and spread her grandma's cozy old quilt over the top as she usually did.

Her husband had left and was living with a younger woman he met at work.

When Gene stormed out of the house after a loud quarrel one evening, Shirley was sure he would be back by bedtime. But he didn't come home, and Shirley didn't sleep a wink all night. He had never stayed away like that.

She phoned him at work the next morning, and he informed her that where he had spent the night was none of her business. Then, timidly, she asked if he had another woman in his life.

"Of course not," he said. "I'm just sick of you."

In a few days, however, Shirley learned from a friend who worked with Gene that the news was all over the office: Gene had moved in with a young divorced secretary. Shirley was devastated! Not only had Gene left her and their two teenage sons alone, but he had gone against all the Christian principles they had held from the very beginning of their relationship.

As she agonized over the situation—her loneliness, pain, and feeling of betrayal, the boys' anger and bewilderment, their financial need, and Gene's comment that he "just had to have a change before he got any older"—she couldn't figure out what had gone wrong. One thing she did know, though. She wanted Gene back. And Shirley believed that God could and would save their marriage!

In spite of her resolve, however, Shirley's emotions ran the gamut in the early days of their separation—shock, hurt, jealousy, anger, depression, then back to shock. Part of the time she was very confused about what to do. Other times she knew exactly what needed to happen and determined to do it. She had strong hopes that things would soon be back to normal.

As the days went by and her attempts to win Gene back proved futile, however, her confidence diminished and her confusion increased. When she appealed to his sense of moral rightness, he said that was a bunch of religious garbage forced on people to try to keep them in line. When she reminded him of their good times together, he growled, "There never were any good times." When she described specific incidents that had been happy for her, he claimed that in his memory the events were nothing but disaster.

When she realized that reasoning with Gene would do no good, she became very frightened. She knew then that their problems were over her head. She asked her pastor to recommend a Christian counselor, and he gave her the name of a professional known for helping people put their marriages back together. Shirley made an appointment. During the following weeks, the counselor suggested ways for Shirley to relate to Gene whenever she got to talk to him. The counselor also advised Shirley concerning changes she needed to make. At first Shirley balked at the insinuation that something was wrong with her. She wasn't the one who had run off. She hadn't been unfaithful.

Eventually, though, Shirley did begin to work on herself even as she practiced the counselor's suggestions for relating to Gene. She believed that her changes would repair their broken marriage.

Her boys and her best friends were all praying with her for God to work a miracle. We, too, were praying for the restoration of Shirley's marriage. We were not the ones directly counseling her, but we kept in regular contact and did our guiding from the sidelines.

Even though communication with Gene didn't go well, Shirley remained undaunted. She had remarkably strong hope that he would come home. In fact, hope was about the only thing that kept her going.

Shirley could never have guessed at the beginning of the ordeal that she would have to "keep up her hopes" for years. *Almost eight years,* to be exact.

During that time Gene continued living with the other woman. They even moved out of the continental United States, which made contact with him more difficult for Shirley. But still she hoped—and prayed—and worked on her personal growth.

When she had nearly reached the end of her rope, she met a woman who gave her some spiritual direction that eventually changed her life. This person told Shirley that God would hear her prayers for Gene only when she let God completely rid her of the garbage within herself. Shirley heard the part about her need for change with only half an ear, but still the conversation renewed her hope.

It took some more time for her to earnestly get to work on her own problems, but finally she came to an absolute dead-end and simply had to let God take complete control of her and start the personal cleansing she needed.

Then one day she contacted us with the joyful news: "Gene has returned!"

We wonder what would have happened if Shirley had given up hope. The circumstances certainly made her confidence appear ridiculous. Most of the people around her thought she was crazy. Many urged her to give up and get on with a new life without Gene. But she didn't listen, and today Shirley and Gene are building a new, stronger relationship.

When Hope Doesn't Work

Hope doesn't always materialize into reality, though. Some people have done everything Shirley did and still haven't seen their marriage restored. Why? The answers aren't easy, and probably no human knows for sure. And certainly no one should heap guilt on those who are unsuccessful.

Some people want very much to save their marriages but simply have no idea how to go about it. Others have let their own anger, hurt, and need for revenge get in the way. But most have tried their very best to do the right things.

We need to realize that God has given us all a free will. And some people stubbornly insist on using that will to walk away from their marriage—in spite of all the good things their spouse does in an attempt to win them back.

We also know that Satan is looking for strongholds. He wants to ruin lives by taking over any space unoccupied by God. And the statistics show he is finding many vacancies!

However, you don't need to let Satan move in on you; you have Christ's power available to help you and your mate keep him out. In fact, praying for your mate is more powerful than anything you can say or do.

God can give your mate a corrected perception of the situation and a desire to change. He can relieve the frustrations that are driving your mate mad, and he can provide an escape from the alluring temptations.[2]

However, it still boils down to the fact that your mate has a free will and may choose to make wrong decisions.

Back to Hope

Despite the gloomy possibilities, the chances of saving your marriage *are* in your favor. The very fact that you are reaching out for help by reading a book like this is a good sign.

Also, God wants your marriage saved. And he's a powerful ally! "When you pour yourself into restoring love to your marriage, you can be sure that *the force of His will is at work with you in the process*" (italics added), says Dr. Ed Wheat, whose books have helped save and enrich many marriages.[3]

It is right to hope. It is therapeutic to hope. You know how depressed you feel when a situation seems hopeless. When you're depressed, you don't have the energy to try. When you don't try, it's like being in a boat without paddles. You'll never get anywhere.

Hope Moves You Forward

We had counseled Karen by letter for over four years, and about a year ago she wrote to let us know that her marriage was once again on safe ground. In a more recent letter she told us that her husband had even asked her to help counsel another couple who is having marital troubles.

She continued, "Isn't it wonderful to know that there is hope in the Lord! That hope, which had never meant much to me before, became the most important thing in my life during the years John was wanting a divorce. What a beautiful work God is doing in us!"

Ted is another person who learned to hope when his wife insisted their marriage was over and convinced him to file for divorce. Their relationship had never been an easy one, but they had shuffled through their conflicts and managed to keep hanging in there with each other.

Ted never told Connie he loved her or appreciated all she did for their family of five children. He did love her, but he certainly saw no need to say it again and again!

When they disagreed about anything, Ted always assumed he was right and never considered Connie's opinion. He usually overpowered her by raising his voice and insisting on doing it his way.

For years Connie let Ted have his way whenever they disagreed, but finally she had her "fill of it." Knowing she could never talk over her frustrations with Ted, she silently started to do her own thing.

She lost weight, got some cute clothes, and went out to see if she could attract other men. She did. And she had affairs with some of them—not so much because she wanted sex but because they listened to her and made her feel important.

When Ted found out, the fur flew! But by then he had lost any chance of influencing Connie. "Our marriage is over!" she insisted. "Just go ahead and start divorce proceedings."

Ted, numb with shock, thought divorce was the only possible outcome, so, for the first time, he did as she asked.

Even after their divorce was finalized, however, Ted couldn't give up hope that they would some day get back together. He ate, slept, and worked with that goal in mind. He talked for hours on end to us, and we guided him through changes he needed to make and suggested things he could do to win Connie back.

Months went by, and Ted kept hoping Connie would see that she had more with him than in her new life. He prayed for her. We prayed for her. And we prayed for Ted to make the necessary changes.

At times Ted wondered if he should just give up and find someone else. Other people were telling him Connie was gone for good. But he just couldn't ignore his all-consuming hope—that one day she would come back.

And hope paid off!

Eventually Connie got sick of the other men and had no place to go. She couldn't afford to live by herself, so, without much fanfare, she quietly moved back with Ted. At first she claimed she was only coming back to keep their family of grown children and grandchildren complete. This is common. A returning mate often does not yet feel "in love" with the other person, but being together gives them a better opportunity to work toward true marital love.

After several months of counseling with us and with their pastor, Connie and Ted were married again. Ted has learned to be more thoughtful of Connie's needs and to respect her right to be heard. And Connie has learned to speak up and not bury her feelings. They now have a strong relationship—and their family is complete!

If you can keep alive the hope that your marriage can be saved, you are ready to start the restoration process. And the first step is to learn what brought you to this place of disaster.

Understand Why This Happened

◆ ◆ ◆

LES DECIDED TO BUILD a storage shed in his backyard, but he didn't want the prefabricated kind; he wanted it to be his own creation. He had never built anything before—except the rickety tree fort he and his brother had nailed together as kids. But he just wanted a simple shed. How hard could it be to build?

After drawing some crude plans and buying some materials and tools, he set to work. He didn't talk with anyone about the project because he didn't want any interference.

Les got the sides to stand up by nailing them onto a frame of two-by-fours. He decided the shed didn't need windows, so he didn't have to measure window frames or cut holes in the walls. The shed did need a door, however. It took Les awhile, but he finally got one installed so it would work. He didn't want to bother learning how to pour concrete, so he decided to have a grass floor.

Building the shed turned out to be harder than Les anticipated, but eventually he got the thing up. It didn't look great, but it was standing. After painting the little building, Les proudly moved in his tools and other items.

One morning after a windy night, Les noticed that his shed was leaning a little bit. No problem. He just went out and pushed it back into line.

The little building got skewed by the wind several more times, but each time Les just pushed it back up straight.

Then one night a fiercer wind blew and a hard rain beat down. The storm lasted all the next day, and the rain washed much of the soil from under the shed. When Les came home from work he found his shed completely down! Everything inside had been soaked by the rain and dented by the collapsing walls and roof.

Don't Cheat Your Marriage

Too many marriages are put together like that little shed. And when the hard times come, they can't stand up. When troubles knock our relationship out of balance, too often we just "push it back up" without making genuine corrections. Then suddenly—or gradually—the whole structure falls apart.

One of the tasks in rebuilding a broken marriage is to determine what caused it to collapse in the first place. In the case of the storage shed, Les thought the wind and rain caused it to fall. The real problem, however, was that the shed was improperly put together in the first place.

External forces did play a part, but buildings can be built to withstand storms. Some expert advice during assembly could have averted the disaster. The materials he used were fine, but he needed additional procedures—such as building a foundation. Even after the shed began to lean, it could have been salvaged and made strong if Les had recognized the problem and asked someone to help him pour a concrete foundation and properly brace the corners.

When marriages begin to totter, many think, *Oh, dear! I've married the wrong person. If I had a different partner, my marriage would be better.*

But you don't need a different spouse; you need new procedures. You probably received little or no counseling at the beginning of your marriage, but there is no reason you can't get it now. You may have developed poor patterns of relating to each other, but you can change them.

Take time to understand why your marriage is falling apart. What is the reason your mate wants to leave? Or has already left? Why is your spouse having an affair? What went wrong since those first days or years when you were madly in love?

It Takes Two to Tangle

A common mistake is to assume that the failing marriage is all the fault of the mate who wants out.

- "He always had a big ego and had to be in control of everything. When I began to challenge that, he couldn't take it and decided he didn't want me around anymore."
- "All she can think about is her own selfish interests. She became obsessed with fulfilling herself and following her dreams. I was in her way."
- "He's always been restless. I should have known that sooner or later he would fall in love with someone else."
- "She's chasing an older man because she needs a father figure."
- "She wants more than any normal man can give a wife."
- "He has a horrible temper and must always have his way. He's finally found someone he can walk all over."
- "He's just like his father. . . ."
- "She's just like her mother. . . ."

The list could go on forever. It always looks like the departing spouse is to blame. The truth is, however, both partners are at fault. There is no completely innocent party. Even the unsuspecting spouse has contributed to the problems. Personalities, temperaments, desires, choices, habits, and all that makes us the people we are, may drive a mate up the wall.

As the years go by, people change. Mates change. And little habits that used to seem like no big deal become as big as Pike's Peak. And the person with the irritating habit may not even realize how annoying it is.

Some people are totally caught off-guard when their spouse announces, "I've had all I can take. I'm getting out." We know of many who thought they had a happy relationship with their mate; the people around them thought the couple had an ideal marriage; and the church even used them as the model couple. It came as a big surprise to one spouse to learn that the other was so unhappy that he or she had already found someone else.

Other partners know very well that they have been a part of the problem. Perhaps they've been too domineering, a nag, a smotherer. Maybe they've been too much of a Milquetoast, never having an opinion of their own, never speaking up for what they believe or want.

Perhaps you are temperamental, rude, or disinterested in what interests your spouse. Maybe you've been sick or grieving and have been unable to meet your spouse's needs. Perhaps you've been negligent in communicating with your mate.

The point is, intentionally or not, you have contributed to your marital problems. It isn't one-sided. Your mate isn't totally at fault—even though that may be hard for you to see right now.

Blindness

Many mates who discover that their spouse is having an affair or is intending to file for divorce learn that they have been blind for years. They haven't noticed that their partner is struggling or unhappy. They have gone through days, weeks, months, even years, totally unaware of the other person's problems.

True, your unhappy mate should let you know that something is wrong, but often he or she doesn't. Your mate feels you should notice without being told. Or maybe your mate feels you wouldn't understand anyway or thinks things are so hopeless that it would do no good to try to talk about them. Some people actually think they are helping their marriage run more smoothly by keeping quiet. Of course, in the long run, the pain is greater than if the problem had been aired and worked out.

Others have tried to tell their partners of their unhappiness, but their words have fallen on deaf ears. An unsympathetic spouse will for some reason fail to tune in or even belittle the problem.

Perhaps you're the one who has been blind or who hasn't been communicating. Maybe you're the one with the hearing problem. In any case, it's time to wake up, find out how your mate really feels, and get to work!

Carelessness

In a troubled marriage usually both partners have been lax about common courtesies. We treat total strangers with more respect than we do the one we promised to love, honor, and cherish. We take each other for granted and often don't realize how rude we are.

People who want to save their marriages must forget about the carelessness of their mates. Rather than expose all the faults of their spouse, they go to work on their own.

Reflect on things you have said or haven't said, or on ways you have reacted or not reacted. Get down to the real reasons for your shortsighted behavior toward your mate.

I* remember how ashamed I was when, after at least twenty years of marriage, I began to see how thoughtless I had been toward many aspects of Jim's character. I had always thought of Jim as being especially tough and hadn't realized how sensitive he was in many areas.

With embarrassment, I recalled times I had stomped all over him, not realizing how tender he was inside. I didn't do it carelessly

---

* In chapters 1 through 20, the use of the first person "I" refers to Sally. In chapter 21, "I" refers to Jim.

or deliberately, but the effects were the same. I had to ask his forgiveness and train myself to be more alert to his real feelings.

Don't be overly hard on yourself, but acknowledge your thoughtlessness and ask God to make you more aware of your mate's needs and feelings. When you get the opportunity, tell your mate you're sorry and that you'd like to become more sensitive to his or her needs. Even if your mate has left or is involved with someone else, saying this may be a turning point in your soured relationship.

Preoccupation

Frequently we contribute to our marriage problems by being absorbed in many interests other than marriage. It's true, life consists of more than marriage and very important "musts" beg to be first on the priority list. But too often we put our mate at the end of the line.

While visiting a friend in the hospital recently we met a very cordial doctor who was making his weekend rounds. He told us of his busyness and even admitted that one Christmas morning he had left home after a brief time with his family and spent all day until after midnight making rounds.

We liked the doctor very much. It was obvious that he delighted in his work and enjoyed giving us a mini-education about our friend's illness. After nearly forty-five minutes with us, he said, "Well, I better be moving on. I have twenty-three more patients to see."

We thought, *If he spends forty-five minutes with each patient, it's going to be long after midnight again when he gets home!*

We couldn't help but wonder how his wife and children felt about his dedication. We were glad that our friend had a caring doctor, but sad that the doctor's family seemed to be so low on the totem pole of priorities.

It isn't just careers that erode marriages; it can be the church, P.T.A., children, hobbies, aging parents, illness, or anything that demands attention.

Sometimes you have no control over things that push their way into your life. If your child becomes seriously ill, you must drop everything and attend to all the details of health care. But while doing so, assure your mate that he or she still has a place in your life and that the preoccupation is only temporary. Vow to once again make your relationship the top priority as soon as possible.

Stress

While evaluating what has gone wrong in your marriage, take a look at the stresses and/or losses you have experienced recently. Often a person whose mate is leaving or is involved in an affair can enumerate a number of difficult things that have happened lately.

Problems at work frequently cause stress that can lead to marital problems. If a person has been laid off, passed over for a promotion, has too much to do, or has a difficult coworker, his or her prestige and identity have been undermined.

A mate with problems at work may come home grumpy and take out his or her frustrations on the family. But there is a more subtle problem. Often the mate under stress feels unable to discuss the problems for fear that his or her spouse won't understand or will be incapable of handling the anxiety.

Affairs have started when a person under stress confides in a third party who gives a sympathetic ear. Often the third party also has needs and is just waiting to get sympathy or "love" in return. In any case, the troubled mate feels this third person meets his or her needs better than the spouse does.

The following list of stresses might trigger your thinking so you can better understand your mate and the reasons he or she wants to run.

- Financial troubles
- Serious problems with aging parents or children
- Moving to a new location
- The death of someone close
- Learning that your children have been sexually molested
- Health problems for you or anyone in the family

- ♦ A car accident
- ♦ Misunderstandings with friends or neighbors

Anything that causes loss or disruption is a potential hazard to your marriage. And, of course, the more of these you have, the more likely you are to have problems.

Even if you only now realize that outside stresses or your preoccupations and actions helped cause your mate to come to the place of breaking your marriage, *it's not too late*. You can't undo the mistakes you've made, but acknowledging your part in the problems is the first step toward healing.

A Word of Caution

Don't use perpetual evaluation as an excuse to delay rebuilding. When you go out to assess why your shed fell down, don't keep kicking around in the debris forever. You'll never get it rebuilt by continually stomping through the broken mess.

Chapter 4

Listen and Speak Selectively

• • •

"YOU BETTER WATCH those two, Tony!" laughed Fred as he gave Tony a hearty slap on the back. "Did you see all the smiles and winks bouncing between Joanne and Herb? Just like the old high school days."

Before Tony's back stopped stinging, another guy came by. "Well, do you suppose you'll ever get Joanne to go home with you now?" he snickered.

Tony was trying to get his wife to break away from a crowd of her former classmates. He had barely been able to tolerate the evening, and these latest remarks made him want to get out as fast as possible. These weren't his classmates; this wasn't even his high school, but he had agreed to come with Joanne because she hadn't been back to her school since graduation twenty-five years earlier.

When Joanne finally was ready to leave, Herb also was leaving. He walked out with his arm around Joanne, and Tony began to seethe. By the time Tony and Joanne reached their motel room, Tony was sullen.

Joanne asked what was wrong.

"Nothin'," he muttered. When they got into bed, he turned his back to her without so much as a goodnight. If there had been another bed in the room, he would have used it.

But Tony didn't go to sleep. Most of the night he mulled over what he should do. Joanne and Herb had talked almost exclusively to each other at the reunion. Tony winced as he recalled how they kept looking into each other's eyes. *So, Joanne had found Herb again and they really hit it off. Just like in high school. Apparently everyone else saw what was going on too. How embarrassing!*

By morning Tony had decided not to fight the inevitable. Joanne obviously thought more of Herb than of him. *They probably have been secretly contacting each other all along,* he concluded. *How could she be so deceitful? And how could she violate our marriage so easily?*

Tony vowed to sleep on the couch when they got home. He would have to start divorce proceedings as soon as he could. He didn't really want to break his marriage; he loved Joanne—but what else could he do? She loved someone else.

Tony was confused, but he thought the Bible taught that a husband was supposed to divorce his wife if she became involved with another man.

Little Remarks Can Make Big Trouble

Tony called a lawyer when they got home, but before actually filing for divorce he called us. He told us he had confronted Joanne and that she had admitted feeling some of the old feelings for Herb. She claimed she didn't want a divorce, however.

We suggested to Tony that just because some feelings had been aroused didn't mean Joanne was being unfaithful or even that she wanted to be unfaithful.

Tony protested. "But everyone could see the interest they had for each other. And I'm sure they're talking about it all over town right now."

Over a period of weeks we guided Tony about how to relate to

Joanne. Fortunately, the couple was able to talk over their situation and make some wise decisions. They each wanted their marriage. Joanne promised not to contact Herb, and Tony agreed not to make accusations. They both vowed to make a greater effort to be open and honest with each other. They decided to begin spending more time together and doing more things to show their love for each other.

Through this near tragic experience, they each learned more about what the other person needed to feel secure and happy. Joanne wanted Tony to spend more time with her instead of working on old cars so many evenings. Tony needed to hear that he was important to Joanne. They were each surprised that the other wanted to be first in ← their mate's life.

Today their marriage is solid. But what would have happened if Tony had continued to concentrate on the incriminating remarks of Joanne's classmates? His doubts and insecurities could have stirred up real trouble in their marriage. Then the gossips would have had plenty to talk about. In fact, the stories probably would have made a divorce more likely.

Don't Believe Everything You Hear

When something goes wrong with your marriage, rumors may fly faster than the wind. Truth may get stretched and bent so badly that only God knows the real facts. Even you and your mate will have different perceptions of the situation.

You've probably lived long enough to know that every person viewing a particular event or circumstance will see it differently. It's like the old poem about the blind men and the elephant. The first blind man approached the elephant, felt its side, and said, "The elephant is nothing but a wall." The second blind man, feeling the animal's tusk, said "an elephant is very like a spear!" The next blind man, who happened to take hold of the elephant's squirming trunk, said, "the elephant is very like a snake!" The fourth blind man reached out and touched the elephant knees and said, "the elephant is very like a tree." When the fifth man touched the elephant, he felt its ear and said, "an elephant is very like a fan!" And the sixth blind man, after grasping the animal's swinging tail, said, "the elephant is very like a rope!"

The stories circulating about your marital situation could be as varied as the blind men's descriptions of the elephant. Each one sees partial truth, but no one sees the whole truth.

That's why it's very important to be extremely selective in what you listen to when people make remarks about your mate.

Even well-meaning friends or family members can be biased. They may have received wrong information or their version of "truth" may have gotten twisted as it came through their thinking and speaking processes. Not intentionally. It's just that humans are fallible in hearing and interpreting information.

But I Was So Sure

Whenever I think of how mistakes can be made from what we *think* we hear, I recall an incident when I was a young pastor's wife. I had quit college to teach a year before getting married, but now we were living in a small town near a church-related liberal arts college and it seemed like a wonderful opportunity to go back to school part-time and finish my undergraduate degree.

We knew our congregation didn't respect this college; in fact, the church believed it was dangerously liberal. Whenever the subject came up, people were very vocal about how many young people had fallen away from the Lord after attending there. They considered it a ruinous place.

Jim and I reasoned that part-time attendance would not harm me. I would not be living on campus; I was a maturing Christian who could not be shaken from my faith; and I was simply taking the classwork to finish my degree. Nevertheless, we didn't broadcast the fact that I had enrolled.

During dinner one evening, the telephone rang and a deacon announced to Jim that the deacon board wanted to come to the parsonage that evening to hold an emergency meeting.

When the deacons arrived, Jim took them to the living room while I washed dishes, played with our two daughters, and folded laundry. Later in the evening I had to walk near the living room to get the ironing board from an adjacent room. Although I was in the room only a few seconds, what I heard set my hair on end! The deacons were talking about me. They didn't want me to attend that college.

The rest of the evening I felt sick to my stomach. My emotions were so churned up I couldn't think clearly, and I'm sure I ironed wrinkles into all of Jim's shirts. I didn't want to disappoint the people of the church nor damage the church's reputation, but I longed to finish my college education. I could hardly wait for the meeting to end.

When the deacons finally left, I said to Jim, "Well, they don't want me going to that college, do they?"

"What are you talking about?" he asked.

After explaining that I hadn't planned to listen in, I described the part of the conversation I had overheard.

Jim stood for a moment in shocked silence. Then he explained that the men never mentioned my name in the meeting! The deacons had come to discuss what to do about an elderly woman who was being severely beaten by her husband. It was a second marriage for both; their first spouses had died. Even though this new husband seemed very pious in public, someone had learned that he was abusing his wife and the deacons believed it was dangerous for her to stay in the home. They were deciding how to get money to help her live elsewhere. I overheard them say, "We want her out of there."

You can imagine how foolish I felt. Where did I get the crazy idea that the deacons were talking about me? And that they wanted me to quit college? I was *sure* I had heard words to that effect.

That incident has been a good lesson to me: *Not everything I think I hear is what is being said.*

You may need to remember that principle when people come to you with stories about your mate. They may not deliberately slant the truth, but be cautious about believing it all. You need a giant strainer.

Instead of simply taking in all the information you hear, filter it through what you already know about your partner. Separate the lies from the truth.

On the Other Hand, Don't Be Stupid

Sometimes, though, it pays to at least consider what you are hearing about your mate. If someone hints that your spouse is seeing someone else, it would be wise to check out the facts. If you think there is any truth to the story, talk it over with your husband or wife.

Your mate may get very angry, and that's scary. But waiting for the truth to finally emerge can be even more scary—and more painful. If you handle the matter kindly and your mate is innocent, the initial anger or hurt will subside. Then you can begin to rebuild trust.

But if your mate is a good liar, he or she may give a very convincing explanation. You'll have to decide whether to believe your mate or your informant. In most cases, it is best to give your partner the benefit of the doubt until evidence to the contrary becomes overwhelming. You probably won't be fooled for long if your mate is trying to deceive you. Truth eventually will emerge.

The Other Side of the Coin

Besides using discretion about who and what you listen to regarding your mate, be exceedingly careful about what *you* say and to *whom* you say it. We've known people who have ruined their chances for winning back their mate by the overuse of their mouths.

When Todd told Lynne he didn't want to be married to her any more, she shared the news with her Bible study group the very next morning. Of course Lynne was upset that he wanted to leave and she needed the support and consolation of friends. But she said *too much too early* and to *too large* an audience.

When Todd moved into his own apartment a few days later, the whole church learned about it. Todd worked at the same place as a couple of other guys from church, and he sensed right away that they knew he had left Lynne.

The entire church talked about Todd and Lynne's problem. For weeks it was the main topic at every prayer meeting. Everywhere Todd went, he ran into people who knew about his marital trouble. And they all either preached at him or ignored him. He felt like a leper with his flesh falling off right in front of their eyes.

As time went on, Todd began to wish he could rebuild his relationship with Lynne, but whenever he tried to see her he felt as if a bunch of other people were in the room with them. He heard all their words of advice floating out of her mouth. She quoted everyone from the preacher to her mother's cleaning woman's aunt. She had been talking and listening nonstop to everyone she knew.

Lynne asked Todd to attend church with her again, but he couldn't bring himself to do it. He didn't have the strength to face all the "judges" at church.

Lynne made church attendance a test of Todd's intentions. When he couldn't muster the nerve to attend, she decided their marriage would never work. In the end, they divorced.

If Lynne had quietly chosen a wise friend or two with whom to confide her pain, she might have saved her marriage. She mistakenly chose to enlist everybody she knew to pray for Todd. She also wanted them to sympathize with her and to ally themselves with her against Todd. She got people's support—but lost her husband.

When choosing how to share your marital troubles, we suggest the following:

1. Tell only one or two people. And choose people you know will keep the matter absolutely confidential. If you are in a small care group that is very close, you may choose to tell the group. But be absolutely certain you can trust each one of them *not* to talk outside the group.

2. Choose wise people. Older people who have experienced the good and bad of life will be able to give you a broader perspective than your peers. Friends who are walking closely with God will probably give wiser help than friends who are not in touch with the Lord.

3. If possible, choose people who can pray effectively. More will be accomplished inside your wandering mate by the power of the Holy Spirit than by all the wonderful words and tricky techniques people can devise.

4. Choose people of the same sex. If you are part of a small care group of couples you've known for a time, you may want to share with all of them. But we warn you not to tell your troubles to one person of the opposite sex unless it is your pastor or a trained counselor. Mates who initially want to save their marriage have often fallen into an affair themselves because they were vulnerable to the attentions of a "comforter" of the opposite sex.

5. Don't wear out your supporters. Yes, you are hurting. And, yes, you need the help of others, but be considerate of them and their families. Before dropping in and staying for hours, ask if it's a convenient time. If a friend says, "I'm always here for you," find out exactly what that means so you don't take advantage of their generosity. Make them promise to tell you when they need time alone or time for other people or projects.

Keep Your Eyes on the Goal

You are in a precarious spot, and you need a few good friends to lean on. But be discriminating about whom you trust. And use discernment as to which stories you listen to and how much you talk about your troubles.

Your goal is to rebuild your marriage. Everything you say and everything you listen to other people say should be done with restoration in mind.

Chapter • 5

Vow to Work Hard

• • •

W HEN DENNIS GOT INVOLVED in an affair he insisted that
his wife file for a divorce, but Bev refused. "I'm committed to
you and our marriage," she explained. "Let's give our relationship a
chance."

Dennis scoffed at her, claiming that their relationship was over.
After a few months, he pressed Bev again for a divorce, threatening
to quit making the house payments if she didn't get a lawyer and start
the proceedings. Bev's friends and family told her she might as well
end the marriage and get on with her life. Even her pastor advised her
to go ahead with a divorce.

Bev tenaciously stuck to her commitment. Although the possi-
bility of restoring her marriage looked extremely bleak, Bev kept
saying, "I have vowed to love Dennis in spite of everything. He is my
husband; I am his wife. We can work on our problems and put our
marriage back together."

It took almost three years, but Bev is one of the happy ones who
achieved what she set out to get. She is convinced that her vow to her
marriage was the one thing that carried her through the times when
it seemed absolutely foolish to go on.

Some marital situations, however, have such major problems

that persistence alone is not enough. If one mate is violent and abusive or using all the family finances to support addictive behavior, the other mate needs to take dramatic steps for protection. As we discuss in greater detail in chapter 15, there may need to be a period of separation while both mates are in consistent, competent counseling. After both mates, especially the abusive one, make significant changes, they can begin to work on rebuilding their marriage.

Commitment

If you have decided your marriage is worth saving, it is time to take the next step, which perhaps is the most crucial of all—an all-out, true-grit *pledge* to keep your marriage. This commitment will be the foundation for everything you do and for everything you are likely to endure in the following weeks.

Initially, you are simply getting your emotional balance after learning that your marriage is in serious trouble. But now you need to buckle your seat belt for the long road ahead.

You won't like to hear this, but it will probably take months—maybe years—to put your marriage back together again. That's why it's imperative that you decide now whether or not you want to be married to your mate. Otherwise, when the going gets rough, as it surely will, you might toss out the whole idea of rebuilding your marriage.

Use Your Resources

Bev's experience may sound like a fairy tale with a happy-ever-after ending, but that's not how it was. You need to know that she worked hard—*really hard*.

Even though Bev vowed to save her marriage, she knew she couldn't do it on her own. God didn't make her to be the Lone Ranger. The commitment did have to come from her alone, but she needed other assets to draw on for the day-in, day-out work of rebuilding her marriage.

She realized she probably wasn't going to get any cooperation from Dennis. He wanted to be rid her. She knew she might also have to work against the tide of others' opinions and advice. Refusing to listen to the antagonists, she found some allies.

Your Greatest Help

Bev wrote and called us many times asking for encouragement for another day, strength for another step. Besides giving her words of hope, we prayed with her and steered her to a serious and regular reading of the Bible. Sometimes our encouragement was as simple as reminding her that

> GOD is on your side. He is the one who planned marriages and families. He also intended that marriage be monogamous, despite the lifestyles of some of our Bible heroes. Therefore, whoever tears and destroys marriages is doing so against the will of God; whoever works at building and reunifying a marriage relationship is pleasing God.
>
> Not only does the Lord think it's a great idea that you want to save your marriage, he wants to give you the wisdom and the power to do the job. You don't have to depend on your puny human strength, which will run out very quickly.

We continued to remind her:

> When you don't know which way to turn or which words to speak, ask God the Holy Spirit to guide you.[1] When you think you can't take another step, ask for his energy to keep you going.[2] God, as a devoted parent, truly cares for you.[3] If you can remember his concern for you when you're feeling down, perhaps it will be the nudge you need to lift your chin again. The King of the universe loves you!

Hundreds of people like Bev have told us that if it hadn't been for the Lord's loving hand holding on to them during the rough time after their mate's departure, they wouldn't have made it.

After Dennis moved out he did cruel things to Bev to force her to file for divorce. He would call to say he wanted to meet her at their favorite restaurant and then not show up. Once Dennis promised to meet Bev and the kids at his parents' house for his father's birthday dinner. He never came.

He would promise to buy new tennis shoes for the boys, but never follow through on his word. He quit making the car payments, although he had said he would make them.

Eventually Bev realized that Dennis was doing these things to test her commitment to take him back. So the more he hurt her, the more she leaned on God to help her keep working on their marriage.

On one occasion Bev wrote, "God has become my very best friend. I find myself praying all the time as if I were talking to a companion right beside me. His words in Scripture are like finding treasures tucked away just for me. I've underlined my Bible so much that I've practically worn it out. Sometimes God's promises are all I have to support me. I would never ask for this kind of pain, but it has driven me to a closer relationship with the Lord, which I wouldn't trade for anything."

Books, Magazine Articles, and Tapes

Other resources are any book, article, or tape that presents concepts to strengthen your marriage. The subject doesn't even have to deal directly with marriage; it could be about some part of the marriage relationship, such as effective communication or successful conflict resolution.

The advantage of books and tapes is that you can read or listen at your convenience and interact with the ideas at your own pace. You also can read and listen as often as you want to parts that are particularly helpful.

For a list of authors and our reading suggestions, see the Recommended Reading section, which appears after the notes in this book.

Counselors and Pastors

A wise pastor or professional counselor can help give you stability during this time. Competent pastors and counselors will aid you in getting a clearer perception of yourself and your situation.

Don't expect easy answers, but do expect to receive guidance so that you can work toward a resolution of your marital problem. The counselor may help you get rid of emotional baggage from your past and help you in areas where you need to grow.

Plan to see your counselor for several sessions. You didn't get into this predicament overnight, and the process of healing will take time. But you will probably begin to experience little changes and some relief from your pain after the first few visits.

Chapter 9 contains more help in how to choose a counselor.

Support Groups

You may be fortunate enough to live in an area that has a support group for people whose mates are in affairs or seeking divorce. Unfortunately, these groups are still scarce. Most community organizations and churches lack either the necessary staff or the courage to admit that such a group is needed.

Some people have found groups such as Al-Anon or another form of recovery group to be helpful. Proceed cautiously in this area and check out the group that you think is appropriate. Don't commit yourself until you're sure it will provide the right influence.

We warn against joining a divorce recovery group. Our experience has been that these groups, naturally, do not focus on marriage restoration and may in fact cause you to quit trying with your mate. Divorce recovery groups are great for the divorced. But if you're not yet divorced and want to recover your marriage, find a group that will give suggestions and support for rebuilding your marriage relationship.

Friends and Family

Your friends and certain family members may be important

sources of strength during this time. Rely most heavily on the ones who are unbiased. You don't need people jumping to your side, pitting you against the "wretch" who wants to break your heart.

Prejudiced friends can fill your head with more negative ideas than you can combat. We see too many people wrongly influenced against their mate because of the words and attitudes of close friends and family members who are trying to console them.

You do need emotional support and comfort, but not at the expense of balance. Tell your friends and family at the very beginning that you want them to be fair and to remain impartial in their judgments.

We have already talked about the danger of revealing your marital problems with too wide a circle so that your mate has an impossible hurdle to cross when he or she wants to come back. Choose a few wise people to be your confidantes and draw on them for the emotional support you need.

If you are in a situation where you need help such as child care, transportation, or even finances, don't be afraid to accept it when people offer. Not only is it good for you, it is also good for them. They get to live out the biblical direction to "bear one another's burdens,"[4] and you get some relief from your problems. God doesn't intend for you to struggle alone; he plans for someone to come alongside to help.

Legal Assistance

Even though we suggest caution about getting the gears of legal action turning too quickly, we recognize that some situations call for an attorney's advice to protect you and your children, especially in financial matters or potential custody cases. Try to get an attorney with a reputation for helping marriages get back together, not one whose clients always end up with a divorce.

If you see a lawyer for legal protection, beware of burning bridges that you may later want your mate to cross. Get the counsel you need without setting into motion anything that will hinder the restoration process.

Take a New Grip—Again and Again

Day after day you will need massive amounts of *patience*. You can't have all you're going to need stored away in some big container; there isn't one big enough. So for each day and for each unpleasant incident, you must depend on God to provide a fresh supply. But you must not let "your rights" and "your lawful needs" clog the channel. While not allowing yourself to be used as a doormat, you do need to say to yourself, "For now I'll turn the other cheek and walk the extra mile."

If time drags on with no sign of progress, or perhaps even a setback—your mate moves in with the other person, cuts off contact with you, blows up at you, or pushes anew for a divorce—be patient. When others urge you to get rid of your unworthy spouse, be patient.

Paint a mental picture of you and your spouse together again and keep it in mind when everything looks bleak. That picture represents your goal—a new, growing relationship that will be a joy to both of you.

Do you want your marriage? Is it worth all the trouble and pain you may have to go through to salvage and rebuild it? If so, now is the time to vow to work toward restoration—even if it takes years and unbelievable amounts of unconditional love. As Bev did, you may need to work very hard and call on every available resource. But you also may get to see your marriage restored, as Bev did.

Chapter 6

Handle Your Mate's Affair Wisely

• • •

YOU'VE JUST CONFIRMED the awful fact that your mate is having an affair! It may be a complete shock, or perhaps you've been suspecting it for some time. In any case, *you are devastated!*

You may feel indignation, anger, or perhaps even guilt if you are wrestling with the troubling thought that the affair is your fault. You may be depressed or vowing to get even. You may throw yourself harder into your work or other projects, or you may be unable to get moving at all. You may feel sick to your stomach or cry easily.

Before this is resolved you probably will feel all these emotions.

You have been betrayed! Your sacred marriage has been trampled on like so much dirt. What do you do next?

Go Carefully

Take time to catch your breath. If you are in a state of near panic, reread chapter 1 before you do anything foolish. Now is the time to act *rationally*, not rashly. Don't force your mate out of the house and don't start divorce proceedings. If adultery has been committed, you have every legal and biblical right to divorce, but God doesn't say you *must* divorce.

In the first few days, spend time asking God for wisdom and peace. Quietly take stock of your situation. If possible, talk to your mate. Don't demand to know details, but do offer to work on solutions. You may feel so hurt that you can't see your fault in the problem, but these things "don't just happen. Every action has a cause."[1] You may not be the direct cause of your mate's infidelity, but you can help make a better marriage that your mate will want to come back to.

Whatever you do, don't make decisions you'll later wish you could reverse. Take time to consider the outcome of any action you might take. For instance, you could:

1. Shoot your mate or the third party—or both. **But** you'd end up in prison and still lose your marriage. Murder is not a good solution.

2. Get revenge. You could put sugar in their gas tanks or make anonymous, threatening phone calls. **But** revenge often backfires, and your anger will probably give you ulcers and drive them closer together.

3. Have an affair yourself. **But** then you'd be guilty of breaking your marriage vows, and your conscience will eat you alive. Also, your mate may accuse you of violating your marriage and sue for a divorce.

4. File for divorce. **But** if you go through with it, you would be left without your mate and with a depressing sense of failure.

5. Work on restoring your marriage.

We, of course, are pushing for number 5, and we'd like to help you through the process.

Understand Why

Your mate may say, "I didn't choose to have an affair; it just happened." But the truth is, your mate *did* have a choice and chose wrong. At some point your mate knew the involvement was headed in an improper direction and failed to stop it.

However, to simply condemn the affair as evil and not discover what went wrong won't solve anything. There are reasons why your mate was easy prey for the devil and if you don't work to correct the causes, your mate will probably continue the affair or begin another.

Christie went to her pastor for help when she found out her husband, Tim, was having an affair with a woman in the church. The pastor was a take-charge kind of man and demanded to know the other woman's name. When Christie mentioned it, the pastor immediately picked up his phone and telephoned the other woman's home.

A male voice answered, and the pastor recognized it as Tim's.

"Tim, what in God's name are you doing there?" roared the pastor. "I want you to get out of there this very minute and don't you ever go back! Do you hear?"

Tim promised to leave and he did. But the pastor never helped Tim and Christie with their marriage. No one explored with them the reasons for Tim's unfaithfulness. Tim and Christie closed the book on that chapter without working on the source of their problems. In a few months Tim was in another woman's bed.

In *The Myth of the Greener Grass*, J. Allan Petersen says, "The affair is a sign of a need for help, an attempt to compensate for deficiencies in the relationship due to situational stress, a warning that someone is suffering."[2]

The reasons for infidelity don't fall into distinct categories; they overlap a great deal. And one inadequacy or condition can cause a chain reaction.

Sexual Addiction

Many women think their husbands are sex addicts because sex seems to be on men's minds so much—or at least that's the myth. True sexual addiction is very complicated, however. The sex addict is never satisfied and is usually involved in many kinds of unhealthy and ugly sexual pleasures. He is constantly driven by his compulsion.

Besides a relationship with his own wife, the sex addict gets kicks from lots of other women—either literally or in his mind. He uses pornographic magazines, videos, or films. He visits places of ill-repute. Wherever he walks or drives, he is always looking, looking, looking.

In fact, he often drives for hours just to enjoy "the sights." Many men talk about women they see at the beach, in the park, or on TV, but the addict is obsessed with women day and night, week in and week out.

Some women are also sex addicts. Their compulsions are as distorted as those of men. Sex addicts need the right kind of help. Reading a Bible verse about lust to them won't cure them. They need a counselor who has successfully treated other addicts. And they also need a mate who will see a counselor and be willing to stand alongside them while they work on the addiction.

Scripture is very clear about the seriousness of sexual sin.[3] It leads to bondage, and addicts are slaves bound tightly with ropes they cannot cut or wiggle out of. Their own will is definitely involved, but it has been so warped that only professional help will get it straightened.

Childhood Damage

Marie's parents neglected her as soon as she was able to fend for herself. Each new baby born into the family got attention only until the child had learned basic survival skills. The children always had enough food, but they had to prepare it themselves. Their clothes were few, but sufficient. What caused the most damage, however, was that none of them got tender nurturing from either parent. Marie's mother, because of her own deprived childhood, knew very little about taking care of children and even less about loving and valuing them. And in those days fathers weren't expected to take much interest in their children; they spent most of the time away from home making a living.

Marie grew up thinking her family was normal. But as an adult she began to feel a void she couldn't explain. She married, thinking that would fill the emptiness, but still something was missing. She gave lip service to her husband, but she always kept her eyes open for someone better.

She finally met a man who listened to her and told her how wonderful she was. She tingled all over and thought she had found true love. When he arranged secret meetings and made clandestine phone calls, she eagerly participated.

But eventually the empty feeling returned. The affair only added gnawing guilt to her lonely void.

When her husband learned of her involvement he was terribly hurt. But whenever Marie tried to break it off with the other man, he too was hurt and always managed to pull her back to him.

Marie was so miserable she finally went for professional help. In counseling she learned how much she had missed in childhood and how it was affecting her as an adult. The counselor encouraged her to grieve over her childhood losses and helped her fill some of the gaps in a healthy way. Eventually Marie no longer needed her lover and stopped looking for "something else."

To help you understand your mate or yourself better, consider the following causes of childhood damage:

- Neglect
- Abandonment
- An alcoholic family
- Family "secrets"
- Physical abuse
- Sexual molestation or attack
- Emotional battering
- Extreme poverty

False Expectations

People today are fed a lot of fantasies and lies about love. We expect marriage to be like love scenes in the movies—constantly full of sizzle and excitement. We forget that movies follow a script carefully created to make the story go just right.

In the real world, where we live, a lot of ordinary, routine living takes place. That doesn't mean we shouldn't experience romance, but we can't expect moonlight and roses every moment we're together.

Unfortunately, many couples enter marriage expecting a fairy-tale relationship. When they find out their mate has body odor, contrary viewpoints, and a selfish streak, they believe they've made a mistake. So they renew their search for the ideal lover.

Cultural Domination

The United States Declaration of Independence guarantees every citizen the right to "life, liberty, and the pursuit of happiness," but people today take the pursuit of happiness to a dangerous extreme. Many believe they have a right to be happy no matter what it costs or whom it hurts. A subculture of Christians and others with high moral standards holds out for marital fidelity, but almost everything we see on television or in movies, books, magazines, and newspapers makes the opposite look more attractive.

Not only do we see a lot of immorality, we are led to believe that nothing is wrong with it. In fact, we're made to look crazy for believing that old stuff about God's design for purity and marital happiness.

Therefore, when a mate is struggling with inner values and external conduct, it's easy for him or her to succumb to cultural standards because they endorse our own selfish desires.

Misunderstandings and Miscommunications

Marital infidelity also can occur when couples constantly disagree or have not learned effective ways to talk to each other. This causes them to lose all trust and respect for each other until finally they see no value in keeping themselves solely for the other.

Sometimes a mate is under a lot of pressure from a difficult situation and feels that his or her spouse wouldn't understand. Quite innocently, the person shares the burden with someone of the opposite sex, and the problem becomes a common bond which may grow into an emotional or sexual affair.

The Specter of Aging

Many affairs happen because of a need to prove oneself young and attractive. Women, as well as men, use sex to demonstrate that the aging process is having no dismal effects on them. They believe that sexual prowess will ward off wrinkles and thinning hair—or at least prove they are unimportant.

Attempts to appear youthful often begin with wearing fashions of the young. And no wonder: catalogs don't show many flattering clothes for anyone over age twenty-five. Few forty- and fifty-year-olds exist in advertising. And if they do, they're modeling "plus" sizes or trying to squeeze into stuff for twenty-five-year-olds. That may be one reason people fight growing older.

People discontented with their age also prefer the company of younger people and youthful activities because people their age or older remind them of the inevitability of aging. It isn't bad to spend time with a younger group except when it's done to try to escape from the reality of aging. The clock can't be stopped even by the best denial gimmicks.

Sagging Esteem

Some people get involved in affairs to prove their value. The victim of low self-esteem thinks, *If I can make that person love me, I'll know I'm worth something—I've really got it, after all. Or, I'll let myself be enticed by this stunning creature who makes me feel young and attractive.*

If you suspect that low self-esteem may have something to do with your spouse's affair, take comfort in knowing that the boost in self-esteem from affairs doesn't last. And when it dies down you can help your mate escape the affair by making it your goal to build his or her self-esteem. Chapter 11 tells how to do it.

Living with the Daily Nightmare

You probably want to step in and put a halt to your mate's affair immediately! That's understandable, but if you go in like a bulldozer you'll ruin everything, even what's good, and be left with no materials with which to rebuild your relationship.

Perhaps someone has even hinted that you are condoning the sin if you don't take a stand against such evil behavior. Actually, you aren't ignoring wrong by taking the inconspicuous approach. You intend to see the violation end. But you want to accomplish it in a way that will most likely insure the realization of your goals, which, by the way, are:

- ♦ To help your mate get disentangled from the affair
- ♦ To correct what has gone wrong in your relationship
- ♦ To build a new, strong, happy relationship

You won't achieve these goals by force. Nor will you accomplish them by inactivity. Pretending that nothing has happened or giving in to feelings of helplessness are not effective responses either.

Pray Like Never Before

If you have not already poured out your heart to God about your situation, now is a good time to start. Many people tell us they never spent as much time praying, day and night, as they did while their mate was being unfaithful. As a result, they found God to be their best friend.

"But," you may protest, "if God cares about me, why did he let the affair happen in the first place?"

As we mentioned before, God allows us to make choices—otherwise, we would be mere puppets—and often we make poor choices. God grieves more over your mate's sin than you do. He provided a way to escape,[4] but your mate didn't take it.

So you and your best friend, God, can talk over your awful situation. Happily, the Lord can do more for you than any human friend. He can give you peace as well as wisdom to say the right words and strength to perform the right actions. He will take all the hurt you hand to him.[5] And the Holy Spirit will move and work in you and in your mate—and even in the third party.

Appropriate God's Promises

Reading Scripture is one of the best ways to calm your agitated heart and to understand more about God. Find a translation that is easy to understand. Underline the verses that speak to you so you can find them easily. Memorize key phrases or verses so you can have the ideas with you all the time. Maybe you want to jot them on a card to keep in your pocket or purse or on the refrigerator or your desk.

The epistles of the New Testament, starting with Romans and ending with Jude, contain many rich thoughts and challenges. If Romans and Hebrews are too heavy right now, read and re-read the others. The Psalms, Proverbs, Isaiah, and Jeremiah in the Old Testament also contain a treasure of help and reassurance. For example,

> For I know the plans I have for you, says the Lord. They are plans for good and not for evil, to give you a future and a hope (Jeremiah 29:11 TLB).

> When you go through deep waters and great trouble, I will be with you. When you go through rivers of difficulty, you will not drown! When you walk through the fire of oppression, you will not be burned up—the flames will not consume you. For I am the Lord your God, your Savior (Isaiah 43:2–3 TLB).

Be Perfect

Of course, you can't be perfect, but your mate expects you to be. While your mate is comparing you to the third person and considering which way to turn, you won't be allowed one misstep.

Dr. Ed Wheat, in *How to Save Your Marriage Alone*, says:

> This [the need to be "perfect"] may come as a shock to you, but if you want to save your marriage, you cannot be just a "good" husband or wife. You have to be perfect in your behavior toward your partner. You must *do* and *be* everything the Bible prescribes for your role in marriage, and you must be very sensitive to avoid anything that will set your partner off. The least slip in word or action will give your mate the excuse he or she is looking for to give up on the marriage. Since resentment and rationalization are two of the key issues in the thinking

of an unfaithful partner, even one remark spoken out of turn can fan the flames of old resentments and give weight to rationalizations that the partner is manufacturing to excuse his or her behavior.[6]

This wise counselor stresses what we all know: we can't be perfect in our own strength. Any good we do or say will have to be by God's sufficiency as promised in 2 Corinthians 12:9–10: "He [the Lord] has said to me, 'My grace is sufficient for you, for power is perfected in weakness.' Most gladly, therefore, I will rather boast about my weaknesses, that the power of Christ may dwell in me. . . . for when I am weak, then I am strong" (NASB).

In working to save your marriage, Dr. Wheat also advises that you must:

1. Consistently do everything you can to please your mate and meet his or her needs and desires (while not violating your moral values or personhood).

2. Show your mate the respect and honor commanded in Scripture whether your mate personally merits it or not.

3. Totally avoid criticism of your mate.[7]

Tough orders to fill. But lots of successfully restored couples can tell you the ideas work.

Write and Burn

There's something therapeutic about writing, and putting your grief on paper may help you live with the distress of your mate's unfaithfulness. Write down what you know or suspect, how that makes you feel, prayer requests about the situation, and anything else that helps you. Pour out your whole heart, and write until you feel some relief. Then burn it all. You don't want anyone else reading your very personal notes. So after each session, get rid of what you've written.

Allow Yourself a Cry

It's better to pour out your agony than to keep it bottled up.

Stifling your feelings could lead to a violent explosion that you can't control, and suppressing tears may lead to physical ailments such as headaches, ulcers, or skin disorders.

Although it's important to let out your feelings, you need to be careful where and how you do it. Cry all you need to, but not in front of your mate or your children for now.

Enlist a Friend or Counselor

Although you shouldn't air your marital troubles to everyone, neither should you drag your burden alone. God doesn't intend for you to stand by yourself during this difficult time. Find at least one wise person of the same sex in whom you can confide, or be in regular contact with a counselor.

Scripture says, "Two can accomplish more than twice as much as one, for the results can be much better. If one falls, the other pulls him up; but if a man falls when he is alone, he's in trouble" (Ecclesiastes 4:9–10 TLB).

God will be your best help, but you also need a friend "with skin on." Carefully choose someone who can come alongside and carry part of your load.

As you live one day at a time—leaning on the Lord, letting someone else help you, and growing and changing personally—you will begin to see hope for the termination of your mate's affair.

Part 2

MEET YOUR
MATE'S NEEDS

Chapter 7

Walk in Your Spouse's Shoes

• • •

LAURA FELT AS IF BOB were keeping her in a bottle, and she didn't like it. She wanted to do more than keep a pretty house and be on parade at social functions with Bob.

Bob and Laura's two kids were nearly grown and soon would be totally gone from home. Missy had been living at home while attending a city college but was planning to transfer to a small Christian liberal arts college five hours away. Brad was a senior in high school and had a scholarship to play football at the same college Missy would attend.

Laura had not worked outside the home since Missy and Brad were born. She enjoyed being a wife and mother, but she was beginning to wonder what she would do with her time when the kids no longer needed her.

Two years earlier Laura had decided to use her talent as a pianist to accompany several church musical groups. Bob grumbled about her being gone in the evenings, but he didn't do anything with her when she was home. When he wasn't out with clients, he sat in his chair watching TV. The kids were usually out with their friends, at their part-time jobs, or with the youth group.

Laura wanted to do something productive during the daytime, but didn't want a career in music. She thought about pursuing a degree in nursing so she could provide better care for the elderly in their local nursing home. Or maybe she could go into real estate. That would be a little more glamorous and she could set her own hours. Or perhaps she could open a small boutique, a dream she had had for some time.

She tried to talk over her thoughts with Bob, but he just scoffed. He didn't want her so busy that she couldn't keep up with the housework and his business life. They didn't need the extra money, he argued, and if she couldn't make up her mind what she wanted to do she must not be very convinced she should be working. If she really wanted to work, why couldn't she just decide what to do and get on with it?

The tension between them made Laura nervous and depressed. She felt Bob didn't really care about her enough to listen to her desires. *How can he be so selfish after all the years I've given to him and the kids?* she wondered.

As the time came for Missy and Brad to leave for college, Laura became more despondent. She wasn't eating or sleeping well and couldn't get herself moving during the day. Not only was she going to miss the kids terribly, she felt she was in a cage. Every time she tried to talk to Bob about her ideas they ended up in an argument. She could hardly believe it when the thought crossed her mind that perhaps she should quietly slip away when the kids left for college.

Feel What Your Spouse Feels

As bystanders we can clearly see what Bob needs to do to hold on to Laura. "Hey, wake up," we'd like to tell him. "It's time to listen to Laura's needs for a change. Encourage her to do something creative with her extra time. Help her wrestle with the choices. Realize how lonely she feels with both kids about to leave."

It's easy to see what someone else should do, but what about you?

Are you trying to see life through the eyes of your spouse? Can you feel what it's like to be where your spouse is now?

The same as Bob didn't understand Laura, Carol couldn't understand Greg. He was threatening to leave home, and it seemed totally unreasonable to her when he said he just couldn't stand the pressure of being there anymore. He complained that the minute he stepped in the door at night, Carol was after him to take care of something around the house or make some decision. The kids were a headache too. Their teenage daughter kept the telephone line busy most of the time, and their two younger sons were usually at the dining room table asking for help with homework or in the family room fighting over video games.

Greg lost his temper several times every evening, so he always went to bed feeling guilty about being a rotten father and husband.

Still, he reasoned, *Carol and the kids demand a lot of me every minute I'm around, and they don't even know what I'm going through at work.*

The truth was, his job was more of a hassle than all the problems with his family. He managed to control himself at work even though he had to do the job of two people because an obnoxious colleague spent so much time patronizing the boss. By the end of the day Greg was so frazzled he took out his frustrations on Carol and the kids.

Then Greg's disgusting colleague got the promotion Greg felt sure he would get. He came home more irritable than ever, but no one even asked what was bothering him. *All they need me for is the money I earn,* he grumbled. *At least they could give me a little peace and quiet when I get home at night. This yammering drives me crazy!*

He thought about getting an apartment where he could have some peace and quiet. When he suggested the idea to Carol, she came unglued!

"How could you even consider such a thing?" she cried.

Greg wanted to tell Carol about all the problems at work, but she was too upset to listen. After a few more miserable weeks he rented a small, dingy apartment close to work.

Carol was sure this meant he wanted a divorce, and she insisted they see a marriage counselor. Reluctantly, Greg agreed. During the counseling sessions Greg finally had the opportunity to tell Carol what life was like for him.

She was astonished! For the first time she began to understand Greg's need for peace at home. When she realized what pressures he was dealing with at work, she decided to make their life more serene.

Greg consented to come back.

Carol made a concentrated effort not to remind Greg of all he needed to do as soon as he got home each night. She enlisted the kids to help by keeping down the noise. Their daughter's friends were not to telephone after Greg got home.

As Carol came to understand Greg and acted accordingly, their home quieted down and so did Greg.

Understand Your Mate's Perspective

If you really want to save your marriage, you must learn what it's like to walk in your mate's shoes. After you've walked a mile in them you will have a better understanding of why he or she is struggling with being married to you.

Perhaps all you can think of are reasons why it is a privilege to be bound to you. But with a little reflection you might remember a few teeny, tiny instances when you could have said something in a kinder tone of voice or acted in a slightly more loving way. You might even grimace as you recall times your mate tried to tell you about a problem or an idea and you didn't listen.

And have you considered your mate's childhood and young adult experiences? If you had weathered the same storms perhaps you'd react to life in a similar way.

As you realize that life looks different from your spouse's perspective, you can try to change yours. It's true that you can't exactly understand your mate's thinking, but you can come closer than you are now.

You *are* two different people with two different sets of life experiences. Even if you've been married a number of years, you still have separate events happening to you each day, and you each react differently to those events.

How, then, can you possibly see life from your mate's perspective? You start by making the determination to *be more sensitive* to your spouse and to *develop your empathy skills*.

Sometimes we identify more closely with a character in a movie or on a daytime TV talk show than we do with the person we promised to love and cherish. But by aligning ourselves as much as possible with our mates we can make a stronger connection with them.

"But I don't see life at all the way my spouse does," you may protest. "In fact, I think my spouse is totally off base."

The question right now is not a matter of right or wrong, but of accepting the fact that this is how your mate feels about circumstances (*and* your marriage) right now.

Being empathetic and sensitive doesn't mean that we wallow in the pit with people. It means that we "feel deeply with them" (the meaning of empathy from the Greek word *pathos*). But we don't get mired down in faulty thinking and behaviors. You don't help alcoholics by getting drunk with them, but you do help by caring and seriously trying to meet their needs. And one of their needs may be to get professional help.

How to Develop Empathy

Some people don't have the foggiest idea how to exercise empathy, but it's not all that difficult. You can begin by increasing your alertness, which means you will listen more carefully and be more observant of your spouse's unspoken signals.

The next thing to do is to *use your imagination*. The ability to be empathetic is closely tied to having a good imagination. Pretend you're actually looking through your mate's eyeballs. Mentally get inside his or her head and see, feel, and understand life from that viewpoint. When you deliberately identify with your mate's feelings you will be able to suffer or rejoice with him or her.[1]

When Jim was going through his mid-life crisis, he was questioning the meaning of life, full of self-pity, and very, very irritable. He was frightened about getting old and even more upset that I was getting old. He was tired of all the demands his family and congregation were making on him. He kept feeling the urge to run away and just escape the whole mess.

At first, I couldn't understand why he should be feeling as he did. Life didn't seem futile to me. I didn't feel old. We were only half-way through life and we had a lot of exciting things left to do.

As the months of his agony continued, I sometimes wanted to shout, "Just snap out of it! Grow up! Think of someone besides yourself for a change!"

Fortunately, I didn't say those things. Instead, just before Jim slid into his deepest despair, I asked him what counsel he gave to women who came to him for help with their husbands in mid-life crisis. He mustered enough objectivity to share some of his suggestions with me.

In a nutshell, these are what he had found helpful to the women he counseled:

1. Commit yourself to a **long time** of working through the crisis—perhaps three to five years.

2. Be your husband's **best friend**. Understand what he's going through and attempt to meet his needs.

3. **Listen** when he feels like talking, but let him have space and **quiet** when he needs it.

4. Be a **girlfriend** to him, not a mother. In other words, be fun and sexy instead of naggy or bossy.

Even though I wasn't feeling what Jim was feeling, I decided to try to imagine what he was going through. His shoes were definitely different than mine! He was a successful pastor and counselor and had the looks and vigor of someone younger than his age. I had spent my adult years as a wife and mother, had received little public affirmation, and looked every bit as old as I was.

But I was determined to at least speculate what it was like to be Jim at this time and place in life. I tried to imagine what it would be like to hate getting older. What would it be like to think I was being exploited? What would be the confusion in my mind as I questioned the meaning of life and didn't come up with any happy answers?

I'm sure I never did completely understand his world, but I was able to empathize better than I had previously. In fact, during the process I got more in touch with my own feelings about aging and the purpose of life.

Be Willing to Learn

Another way to understand your mate's world is to *ask questions*. Ask about their views on life—their own lives in particular. Ask what makes them feel happy or fulfilled.

Even if your spouse has left, you can ask questions whenever you do have contact. Ask appropriately, of course. You're not a Gestapo agent trying to force an enemy to talk. You want the experience to be as pleasant as possible.

If your mate is not available for discussion, ask other people who know from similar experiences what your mate is feeling. Piece together as much information as you can to get a picture of your mate's inner struggles.

By showing genuine interest in your mate's world, you will likely detect some softening in his or her determination to get rid of you. In turn, you will learn more about what's really going on in your mate's mind and heart.

Chapter 8

Listen Attentively to Your Spouse

◆ ◆ ◆

SHARON GREETED PETER from the kitchen when he came home from work, but he didn't stop to talk. Later, during dinner, their three teenagers chattered nonstop about school and church events and their friends. Sharon joined in frequently, but Peter remained silent. When a phone call took Julie away from the table, Sharon asked Peter how his day had gone.

"Lousy," he mumbled. It was the first word he'd spoken since coming in the door. He picked up a dinner roll and was silent again.

"My day was hard too," replied Sharon, and she launched into a story about an argumentative customer she'd had at the bank where she worked as a teller. She was still relating the details when Julie returned to the table. The conversation again turned to the kids' interests.

Peter excused himself from the table after he had finished eating. He made a short business call from the bedroom phone and then sat down in the family room and turned on the television. Sharon joined him later. Their only conversation was a discussion of which programs to watch.

As they undressed for bed that night, Sharon rehashed some of her feelings about her irritating customer. Peter, lost in his own thoughts, didn't respond.

After they settled into bed, Peter gave a big sigh and said, "I'm not sure what to do about the mess at work."

"Oh, don't worry," Sharon said cheerily, "you'll think of something. You're tired tonight. In the morning the world will look better." With that, she turned over and went to sleep, leaving Peter to spend the night tossing and turning alone.

Listening to Problems

Many of us go through life not knowing how to listen. We can hold a conversation, but usually we focus on *what we have to say* rather than on *what the other person is saying*. While the other person talks, we think about what to say next and can hardly wait for the opportunity to jump in.

Women complain to us that they can't get their husbands to communicate. When we probe a little into the relationship we often find that sometime in the past the husband did try to say something, but his wife didn't listen and he finally gave up trying. We also find that many husbands don't listen to their wives because they think women talk all the time but not about anything important.

Both these problems are real—but there are solutions.

Although exceptions do occur, men generally use words to take care of business and to solve problems. They tend to get right to the point and very often don't say anything until they have a problem all figured out.

Women, on the other hand, use talking as a form of companionship. They think out loud, letting others share their reasoning process.

The talkative mate could learn a lot about the other one by truly listening to the few words he or she does say and by watching for nonverbal signals. In turn, the quiet spouse could better understand the chatty one by reading between the lines, watching body language, and realizing that all the words are an attempt to connect emotionally.

Peter needed Sharon to tune in on his one word—*lousy*. He might have talked further about his problem if she hadn't jumped in to tell about her bad day. In bed that night Peter again was willing to discuss his dilemma, but again Sharon turned him off by her overly simplistic response.

Eventually Peter quit trying to share his problems at all. Sharon accused him of never communicating because to her communication meant lots of conversation. She didn't realize that the few words he did say were his way of communicating, so she failed to follow up when he tried to get his feelings out.

Unfortunately, Peter found someone who did listen—Penny from work. She genuinely cared about his troubles and told him all the great qualities she saw in him. He hadn't intentionally looked for an affair, but if the relationship continued Peter would likely turn to this woman for sexual satisfaction as well as for emotional satisfaction.

How Do You Really Listen?

True listening is hard work and takes discipline. I have known about active listening (or creative listening, as it is sometimes called) for nearly twenty years, but I still don't have the skill down pat. It is easier for me to talk than to listen. Yet when I do switch into the "listen" mode, I am always amazed by what I learn.

Not only do I find out about the person to whom I'm listening, but often that person finds a solution to a problem or, at least, finds emotional release. When I actively listen to Jim, he often thanks me for helping him see an issue more clearly even though I haven't given him any answers. Just being able to "talk it out" gives him a perspective he didn't have before.

Following are some things we've learned about true listening.

Listening Takes Time

Listening is best done when we stop other activities and limit other noises. This means putting on the brakes, and that isn't easy in our hurried world where we never have enough time to do all the important things that need to be done.

If we really want to know what makes our spouses tick, however, we have to take time to let them talk. We must make listening a high priority. In fact, if we mean business about bettering our relationship, we will make listening our *highest* priority. And listening must be done in non-rushed moments. We can't hurry the process.

Listening Requires Focused Attention

Many events in life do not require 100 percent concentration because our minds can receive more than one stimulus at a time. But if we want to be sure we are catching every bit of the message our mates are sending, we must focus totally on them.

An important aspect of focused attention is eye contact. If we glance around the room, we indicate that something is more important than the person speaking. If we turn away from that person, drum our fingers on the table, or tap one foot, we show that we are bored. To truly connect with people and let them know they are significant to us, we must give them clues with our eyes and the rest of our body.

Not only will we detect the full meaning of what our spouses are saying by focusing on them, we also will give them the assurance that they are important to us. They will sense our concern. Our attention tells them that we'd rather be with them than anywhere else. When they feel confident that they are cared for they will be more likely to disclose their feelings and thoughts.

Listening Means "Be Quiet"

When we want to learn what is really going on with our mates, we have to be quiet and let them do the talking. That's hard when we have so much wisdom to dispense, so many observations to make, and so many experiences to share. However, information is not what they need right now. They simply need a listening ear. A time may come when talk is appropriate, but we need to make sure we've done sufficient listening first.

The Art of "Drawing Out"

When we actively listen to our mates, we may sense they're having trouble saying what's on their minds. They can't find the proper words or aren't sure how much is safe to talk about. If they hesitate, we may think they've said all they're going to say. But that's probably not so. This is the time to practice "drawing out." Try rephrasing the last comment made by your spouse. By assuring your mate that you are listening you can often spur more talk.

Sharon was learning to draw Peter out. One evening she picked up on a single word Peter said: *Penny,* and she suddenly realized he had been mentioning that name frequently. Sharon decided to listen more closely to everything Peter said, no matter how little it was, and to pay closer attention to the clues he was sending her. A few days later Sharon had the opportunity to put her resolve into practice.

"Boy, I sure do dread going back to work tomorrow," Peter said as he climbed into bed on Sunday night.

Instead of assuring him that he would be able to handle whatever came along, Sharon determined to find out more about what was troubling him, so she rephrased his comment.

"You don't want to go to work?" she asked, being careful to make the comment in a neutral tone of voice and softly phrasing it as a question so it sounded neither patronizing nor judgmental.

"Yeah, I have some tough decisions to make," he added tentatively.

Sharon wisely chose not to question him directly. Instead of demanding to know "What kind of decisions?" she simply said, "Decisions?" leaving him free to say as much or as little as he wanted.

Sharon desperately wanted to say something to fill the silence that followed, but instead she kept her focus on him, quietly expecting him to say more. And finally he did.

As Sharon continued to actively listen and occasionally repeat

Peter's last words, he felt liberated enough to continue talking. When Peter concluded, they both felt satisfaction. For the first time in years Peter felt that Sharon cared about the problems he was wrestling with, and Sharon felt as if Peter had let her in on the details of his business life, which he had always told her had "nothing to do with family."

Don't Pass Sentence

A major hindrance to self-disclosure is the fear of judgment. Perhaps the issue with which your spouse is struggling is one you have previously condemned. Knowing this makes your spouse fear that you will be overly harsh.

If he or she is involved in a moral problem, you certainly will have a strong opinion. But at this stage, it is important to convince your spouse that you want to hear his or her viewpoint and that you will listen without condoning or condemning.

If this sounds wishy-washy, we assure you that we are not advocating that you turn your back on your value system. Not at all. We simply want you to recognize that your spouse has the right to be understood and cared for, no matter what he or she has done or is struggling with. Your spouse needs to know that you can listen nonjudgmentally, that you want to understand, and that you care. When the whole story comes out, perhaps you'll have a viewpoint that surprises both of you.

Or perhaps your mate, after verbalizing his or her thoughts or actions, will come to see the situation more clearly. People are more apt to make the right decision, and stick to it, if they make it of their own free will and not because someone is preaching at them or pointing accusing fingers.

Keep Confidentiality

Some spouses are afraid to communicate for fear of what their mate will do with the information. They may be afraid it will be used against them or told to other people.

Our mates' struggles—whether problems at work, fear of the

future, unattainable dreams and goals, feelings of rejection, or temptation—must be treated with the greatest of respect. When they entrust this information to us, it is not something others need to know, nor is it something to use as a weapon against our mates.

No Need for the Shell Answer Man

A mistake people often make is to think they must give solutions to their mates' problems.

- ◆ "If you'd just tell your boss. . . ."
- ◆ "You can find fulfillment by simply throwing yourself more into our home. . . ."
- ◆ "You need to read what the Bible says about that. Here's a verse. . . ."
- ◆ "You should do it like this. . . ."
- ◆ "Just keep away from that woman. . . ."
- ◆ "The next time you see your father, simply say. . . ."

As easy as it is for us—with all our knowledge—to clearly see what our mates should do or feel, our answers are not what will help most at this point. For now we are to be *listening*, not giving wise advice. Before we start talking, we should be very sure we've listened and listened and listened.

When we do finally speak, we must do so carefully. Here again, God's wisdom is crucial.

As Sharon listened while Peter revealed more of his problems at work, she learned that Penny, a woman he had hired a year earlier, was very unproductive and causing a great deal of strife. Peter's boss had told him that he must get rid of her.

However, Peter felt sorry for Penny. She was a single mother with three children and had had a very rough life. This job was one of the best things that had ever happened to her.

As Peter further disclosed his dilemma, he acknowledged that he had become infatuated with her. She often came into his office to talk about her personal problems. He enjoyed talking to her, and he felt good that he had been able to help her.

In fact, he had talked to her about a personal relationship with Jesus Christ and she seemed close to making a decision. If he fired her she might never become a Christian and she certainly would feel that the world, and probably even God, was against her. But if he didn't let her go, his own job was in jeopardy. As he talked, he realized for the first time that his marriage would also be threatened.

He was in a predicament.

Very wisely, Sharon just listened. When he told her of his emotional attachment to Penny, she trembled inside but said nothing. She could have raged, "Get rid of that woman immediately or I'm leaving. Then see where you'll be!" Or, she might have said, "You'd better listen to your boss. How could you possibly blow your whole career for someone who's a liability?"

Instead, by letting Peter talk it out, she allowed him to clarify his thinking and determine the direction he needed to go. He realized his feelings for Penny were based more on sympathy than anything else. He had enjoyed being a rescuer, but she needed to carry her own weight on the job and take responsibility for her personal life as well.

Penny really was a detriment to the company, and he needed to find someone who could make a contribution. This would not only put him in better standing with the boss, but would actually help the entire organization be more productive.

A few days later Peter released Penny—although it wasn't easy—and began searching for the right person. He was much more at peace with himself; he even liked his job better. And it was much more fun coming home to Sharon at night.

"But My Mate's Not Here!"

You may say, "This chapter is fine for those people whose mate is around to be heard, but mine is gone!" Or "How can I practice listening when he only telephones about business matters?" Or "What's there to listen to when all she does is sit in the car while she drops off the kids?"

Jody's counselor gave her a crash course in how to effectively listen to her husband, Phil. Phil had disappeared without much warning and with no indication of where he was going. Jody, of course, was worried sick.

Three nights after leaving, Phil called. "I just want to let you know I'm all right and to see if you are too," he said almost tenderly. When Jody asked where he was, he turned cold and said, "That's my business. And don't ask when I'm coming back!"

Jody's counselor helped her see from that conversation that Phil had actually given her more information than his words alone revealed. He wanted her to know that he was safe and that he cared about her well-being. But he still needed privacy and to feel in control of his own life.

With each subsequent call, Jody received more insight into Phil's inner feelings. She learned to let him talk as he felt up to it. She didn't nag or give advice. He opened up more and more to her and finally offered to come get her for a "date" so they could talk some more.

Phil and Jody's communication certainly wasn't as full as it would have been if he were home and their relationship was healthy. But Jody learned to appreciate all that Phil was saying and meaning whenever they did talk. She found she was getting to know him better than she ever had.

It *is* much harder to listen to your mate when he or she is out of the home. However, unless your mate has completely broken all contact, you can still use the little snatches of time you do get.

When your mate telephones, stops by the house, or meets you somewhere, use the opportunity to genuinely tune in. Yes, you have your hurts and your agenda, but put them on hold for now. Focus your attention on your mate as a true friend would. Let your spouse know you care by listening and practicing the art of "drawing out."

Your mate may put up a front of anger or coldness, but look beyond the facade and try to see the struggle going on inside. Your mate is full of questions and doubts, even though the exterior shows otherwise.

Only God knows your mate's inner workings for sure. But you're aware of enough to know that something's going on and you need to find out more. Don't get angry or let your feelings get hurt because of your mate's hostility or distant emotions. Focus on your mate's needs, not your own.

At this point, these actions and attitudes may seem achievable only by a Super Spouse. Since you're a mere human being, you won't always do and say—and *not* say—everything correctly. But it will help to have listening as a goal you're working toward.

Over time, you will be pleasantly rewarded if you
- ♦ take time to listen,
- ♦ focus attention on your mate,
- ♦ keep quiet so you can hear,
- ♦ draw out your mate,
- ♦ be nonjudgmental,
- ♦ keep confidentialities, and
- ♦ give support rather than solutions.

Chapter ◆ 9

Deal with
Emotional Clutter

• • •

RECENTLY THE TWO OF US cleaned our garage. Somehow the odds and ends we store there always outgrow the space. Some of the stuff just needed to be straightened and rearranged, but most of it needed to be thrown out—cans of old paint, a broken coffee maker, empty boxes, and stacks of plastic plant pots. When we finished the task, we were exhausted, as usual.

You may be in need of some intense emotional housecleaning if your mate is threatening to leave or has already left. The attic, basement, closet, and garage of your mind may be crammed with clutter from the past.

If you're like we were, you may be overflowing with emotional debris. But we didn't see our mess for years. We both had accumulated emotional garbage during childhood and had added to it during our years together. We hadn't had much adult life apart from each other because we were married as soon as Jim graduated from college. But some couples collect a lot of psychological junk during their single adult years.

At first you may have to do the cleaning and digging by yourself. Your mate may want no part of it. But you still have to consider his or her trash, along with your own, because your mate's emotional garbage affects you too.

You may think the task is too big, too ugly, or too painful. Or you may be blind to the mess you are in. The truth is, the longer it goes untouched, the worse it becomes. We wish we had started ridding ourselves of extra emotional baggage years ago, before some of it grew into serious disorders.

Even if you have gone a long time without dealing with your accumulated clutter, it's not too late. It's better to now so you can enjoy the years you have left. A couple we know had a miserable marriage for over sixty-one years. The wife died recently—without either of them ever having tried to work on their problems.

When we realized we had to get to work on the trash piles in our lives, we vowed not to waste any more time. Once we made the decision, Jim kept saying, "This is the year I'm going to get healed!"

He set out to find a therapist in whom he could have confidence. For years he had fought against seeing a counselor, because, as a counselor himself, he couldn't imagine what anyone could tell him that he didn't already know. And whom could he trust? But eventually his childhood pain became so great that he knew he had to find help. After a while I began seeing the same counselor.

Small Care Groups

About the same time Jim began therapy, we each became part of small—very small—care groups. Jim meets with two other men, and I meet with two other women. We can count on these people to listen to us and to keep whatever we share within the group.

Our friends have walked with us through very hard times as we have struggled to get free from the long, ugly tentacles of Jim's childhood experiences, which had severely affected our marriage and even our childraising. Sometimes we have been very difficult folks to be around, but our friends have loved us anyway.

Our friends also share their problems with us, and together we have become a true support for each other. Besides meeting together, we pray regularly for each other, telephone each other several times a week, and have many fun times together. These people have been like lifelines to two drowning people. In the early days they rescued us; now they keep us from going under again.

Time to Work Together

The two of us also began to do more talking and working together to clean out our old emotional clutter. It took time; and it still takes time—often at what seems the wrong time—and sometimes it hurts. But it's certainly worth it.

We have become more honest with each other. It isn't that we lied to each other before; but we often withheld the whole truth or tinted it a little to protect the other one.

We entered the waters of truthfulness gingerly. We didn't dare just plunge in. Little by little, one of us would say something like,

"I'm uncomfortable with what you just said. . . ."

"I'm left with a feeling I don't like. . . ."

"I wonder if I understand what you mean. . . ."

Previously, we would have stuffed the uneasy feelings deep inside and never come to a mutual understanding. We thought we were being Christ-like by not prolonging a disagreement or making the other angry. Instead, we were following patterns we had learned in childhood; and a lot of the misunderstandings and resentments we buried eventually germinated into an ugly mess we couldn't control.

Clutter from Long Ago

Your attitudes about life and patterns of living started forming in childhood. Even if you think you've changed your attitudes and behaviors a good deal from that of your parents, your world is still colored by what did or didn't happen to you as a child.

If you felt loved, valued, and listened to, you have a different picture of the world—and even of God—than if you were neglected, physically or sexually abused, and made to feel unimportant. You may have forgiven those who did these things to you, but those deeds still are part of the accumulation of experiences that makes you who you are.

Often people don't realize that their childhood experiences are still entwined in how they function as adults. Some attitudes and responses can cause strife in marriage without giving a clue as to the source.

For years, whenever Jim came home after a day at the church, I would ask, "What happened today? What did you do?"

If he was in a good mood, he'd answer, "Oh, I can't really remember. The day was so full." When he was in a poorer frame of mind, he'd say, "I don't feel like giving a report." If he was in an even worse mood, he'd grumble, "Why do I have to tell you everything I do? Just let me run things without having to give an account to you."

Many years down the road, we woke up to the influence of Jim's troubled childhood on his adult life and realized why we ran into trouble when I asked about his day.

His mother always suspected that children who were out of her sight were up to no good. She would greet them at the door with "Well, what trouble have you been into now?" Or, "You're five minutes late getting home from school! What have you been doing?"

Jim grew up being mistrusted and falsely accused. So even though I just wanted to know how things were going for him and to show I cared about his world, he heard his mother's inquistions.

Together we worked on the problem. I was more careful in how I asked about his day, and he reminded himself that I was asking because I cared about him, not because I was checking up on him.

If either you or your mate came from a troubled—or dysfunctional—home, you may need a lot of healing. The helpful steps to recovery from a damaged homelife are covered in Jim's book, *Adult Children of Legal or Emotional Divorce*.[1]

Other Clutter

Besides childhood debris, one of you may have rubble left from your adult life before marrying your spouse. This could include:

- A previous marriage or love affair
- Sexual assault
- Multiple career changes
- Military service
- Drug or alcohol addiction or other harmful habits
- Running with the wrong friends
- Living too long with your parents after becoming an adult

These must be dealt with as part of solving your present marital problems. Again, you may need outside help from a discerning counselor who understands dysfunctional families.

If either you or your spouse has been married before, reading books about remarriage and the "blended family" may help you. Insights from others' experiences can give you some tips to work on. Christian bookstores and some church libraries are well-stocked with books on remarriage and how to make new families successful. One book we highly recommend is *When You're Mom No. 2* by Dr. Beth Brown.[2]

Helpful books on addiction and codependency are also available. Some are listed in the Recommended Reading section.

Whatever your problems from your previous adult life or your mate's earlier life, it is important to face them and do what is necessary to put them at rest. They have cluttered your present life long enough.

You can't undo past events—especially if there are living reminders, such as children. So instead of pretending certain things never happened, decide now to face them and find some solutions.

Everyday Clutter

Cleaning away the garbage that has accumulated in marriage may be more difficult than getting rid of clutter from the past because we are less likely to see the mess we have become accustomed to. And even if we do see it, we're likely to blame it on our mate.

You probably have been married long enough to know that *old hurts* sting every time you remember them, and you probably have quite a supply by now.

Connie and Ted, the couple we mentioned in chapter 2 who divorced and then remarried each other, had to work on the emotional destruction caused by Connie's unfaithfulness. For months after they remarried, Ted worried whenever Connie left the house. He was a nervous wreck every time he thought of Connie's past affairs.

Finally, he came to the place where he knew he had to put all that behind him. Connie assured him of her loyalty and asked again for his forgiveness. When he specifically uttered the words, "I forgive you," he found a release.

Certain words or events may always activate memories of a grievance or start a new argument with your mate, so it helps to recognize these *triggers* and be on guard. If you can identify them and see them coming, you can prepare yourself and avert the usual consequences.

Secrets are another cause of damage in marriage. This doesn't mean Christmas or birthday surprises; it means withholding information that should be general knowledge between you and your mate.

Art and Susan had been married for over twenty-five years, yet Susan never knew how much Art made at his job. For years he kept the bank account in his name and gave her an allowance. When she got a job outside the home and started a bank account of her own, Art expected her to pay most of the household expenses from her earnings.

Several times during their marriage Art bought a new car and proudly drove it up in front of the house, expecting Susan to be delighted. She hadn't even known he was thinking of changing cars, and he never let her be involved in deciding the make or color.

Recently Susan discovered they had heavy debts and were in danger of losing everything. Art had wanted to keep the details to himself, but he was managing so poorly that he had to divulge some of his secrets. And Susan had to take a crash course in finance management and jump in to salvage what she could. The whole experience caused a great deal of division between the two of them. In fact, Susan's emotions were so on edge that she asked Art to move out for a while.

It's time to get those hurts, trigger events, or secrets cleaned out and make room to live life to the fullest! Left unattended, emotional garbage will take it's toll—sooner or later—on our physical well-being. The result may be headaches, ulcers, chemical imbalance, heart problems, or other diseases. Emotional tension saps our immune system so that our bodies cannot effectively fight infections and other ailments.

If you're beginning to see the garbage for the first time and think that you can get along by just covering it up, you're only adding to the mess. You can go on stumbling over it for a time, but how much better it would be to have an uncluttered, healthy, fun marriage!

Getting Help

To get rid of the junk in your marriage, you probably will need the help of a competent counselor. Look for one with at least a master's degree in psychology or in marriage, family, and child counseling (MFCC) from an accredited school. Therapists with a doctorate in marriage and family counseling are even more qualified to help you.

Education, however, is not the only guide. You will want a therapist whose values do not conflict with your own. You may want a Christian counselor, but keep in mind that being a Christian doesn't guarantee ability.

Choose a counselor known for helping couples put their marriages back together. Some therapists emphasize individual growth and independence to such an extreme that they actually encourage divorce rather than restoration. Other counselors become discouraged when a marriage doesn't heal quickly and begin to recommend divorce.

If either you or your spouse is also working on recovering from an unhealthy childhood, find a therapist who understands dysfunctional families.

For our own counselor we are pleased to have found a well-educated, well-qualified Christian who grew up in a dysfunctional home. Most of his clients are working through problems from dysfunctional childhoods.

Don't be afraid to ask questions about the person you are considering as a counselor. You have a right to know about the person's education, particular specialty, and personality. When you telephone the therapist's office, tell the receptionist that you are gathering information to make a decision about choosing the best counselor for your needs. The process should include a telephone interview with the counselor.

You also need to ask about the cost of counseling. If you can't afford the fee, the counselor may offer you a reduced rate. If the cost still is too great, look for a church or community agency that offers free or low-cost counseling. Some health insurance plans cover counseling costs.

In considering the price of counseling, also consider the cost of *not* getting professional help. Remember, a divorce costs a lot of money too—and it leaves you with nothing but a broken marriage.

Don't be afraid to change counselors if after several sessions you don't click with the first one you chose. You need to feel at ease with your therapist or you won't make much progress.

At First It Hurts

We know it takes hard work to dig through the debris in your lives, but you'll be glad for the good changes it brings. "What do you mean—good changes?" you may ask. "Things are worse than before."

Ridding yourself of accumulated junk sometimes causes a great deal of agony in the beginning. It's similar to having an appendectomy. The surgery and recovering are painful, but later you are much healthier than you would be with the rotten appendix.

By anticipating the pain and bracing yourself for it, you will be able to handle it. And knowing that you will eventually see signs of health will help you through the hard times. Little rewards along the way will encourage you on your journey toward recovery.

We knew it was going to be a day of hard work when we started to clean the garage. We got tired and dirty, but we couldn't quit once we had everything pulled out into the driveway. So we kept at it, and when we had finished sorting and had things in place we felt very good. The garage was clean and organized. We could walk through it again. The result was certainly worth the work.

Instead of being left alone with an attic full of old trunks crammed with ugly remnants of your past life, you can be on your way to clutter-free living. And we hope your mate will be with you for the trip.

Chapter 10

Consider the Career Pressure

• • •

K EN WAS A QUIET, gentle man who loved his family, but he was on the verge of leaving them. No one would have guessed it a few months earlier. He had always been a spiritual leader in his church, and many admired him. For over a year, however, he had been so exhausted that he could barely move one foot ahead of the other. But he felt he had to keep going to provide for his family.

He worked extra shifts to earn enough money so his children could have music lessons, attend special activities, and so the family could live in a big house in a nice part of town. The mortgage was a huge drain on Ken's paycheck, but it was a wonderful house—a house where he spent very little time.

Eventually Ken just snapped. He began disappearing from work. He'd get in his car and drive until he ran out of gas. Although devoted to his wife, he became attached to a woman at work. He couldn't understand what was happening to himself. He decided he'd better leave town before he destroyed his family. *If I just disappear,* he reasoned, *it will save my wife and kids a lot of unhappiness. If I stay around here, I'll end up disgracing everyone.*

Fortunately Ken's wife, Ruth, came to us for counseling before Ken left for good. Alerted to his problem, Jim began to drop in on Ken at work. As they became closer friends, Jim learned how tired Ken was from overworking and that he felt confused and unable to make good decisions. Ken's bewilderment had led to the involvement with the other woman, and he felt so ashamed that he thought the best way out of the mess was to get away completely.

Less but More

Ruth continued to come for counseling. She began to see how Ken's many hours of work had brought him to this point. As she and Ken started to talk more openly about the complications, she assured him that she would forgive him for his unfaithfulness even though it had hurt her terribly.

She encouraged him to return to a normal work schedule and agreed to move to a smaller house, get rid of one car, and cut back on some other expenses. The older kids, who had become aware of the potential family breakup, willingly gave up some of their activities and hobbies to have Dad at home. It was hard to share crowded bedrooms, but it was far better than living in big rooms with no father.

Would you be willing to lower your lifestyle to save your marriage? Would your family move into smaller living quarters or do without some other things if doing so would keep your mate from leaving?

Work Equals Significance

My father was a hard-working farmer for much of his life and in later years he became a cabinet-maker. He owned his own shop and put in six long days every week at his craft. As he aged, this work too became difficult and he had to slow down because his legs and arms were becoming weak.

I visited him just before he retired at age 82. One evening while he sat in his big recliner, I perched near him and took his big, gnarly hands in mine. "How are you feeling, Daddy?" I asked.

"Oh, I feel pretty good. It's just that I'm 'no account,'" he replied sadly. "I can't lift those sheets of plywood like I used to, so I'm not much good to anybody."

I could see I needed to let my daddy know right then that he was special to me and the world, even if he couldn't work much.

Our mates also need to know they are of much more value to us than their paycheck or career accomplishments. And we need to stick by them while the tide of outside praise is out to sea.

This does not mean that we should underestimate the importance of our mate's career. We will be of no comfort if we say "Don't let your work bother you—it's not that important anyway! It's just a job." Work is important and our mates want it to run right.

A large portion of a person's identity comes from work, whether it's managing a household or working outside the home. When people are introduced at social or business gatherings, their names are almost always attached to their job identification rather than to their character. We don't say, "This is John Brown, an honest and caring husband and father." Instead, we say, "Meet John Brown, head of marketing at Acme Corporation."

Since work takes up so many hours of each day, we can see why job satisfaction or dissatisfaction affects everything else about a person's life. And families often bear the brunt when things go badly at work. Our niceness batteries last only so many hours—usually while we're at work—and then watch out! Our mean side kicks into action and all disgusting individuals within the four walls are in danger. (And everyone, especially the mate, is disgusting.)

Work Can Mean Destruction

Unhappiness at work can have several effects besides marital strife, including physical problems such as heart disease, ulcers, rashes, digestive disorders, and breathing difficulties. Job stress also accentuates negative emotional tendencies, which create an ever-widening circle of complications.

People desperate to change career circumstances may say something foolish to a boss or coworker that they would not say while thinking clearly. Or distress may cause people to make a poor choice in choosing a new job, grabbing the first available position whether or not it fits.

Job troubles can be anything from too little pay or a poor working environment to disagreeable employers or incompetent employees; from unfair promotion practices to a mismatch in career. Jobs can be too demanding—or too demeaning.

Some work situations tear away self-esteem. And people's value of themselves is greatly smashed when they are dismissed from jobs or can't find a job. Retirement also can be hard on self-worth. Most of us think our value is in "doing," so when we aren't doing we feel worthless.

Some men don't understand their wife's desire for a meaningful career. In the last two decades, many women have abandoned their husbands and children to find "their place." A wise husband will help his wife find fulfillment so she won't want to break the marriage.

For some women, a paycheck is an official sign that someone considers them worthy of reward. An assistant of ours used to say, "Money isn't everything, but a paycheck is one way of knowing you've pleased somebody."

Not every threatened marriage has work and money pressures, but sometimes that's where the trouble starts. And often we don't recognize job difficulties as the source of the friction, assuming instead that the problems are caused by a difficult mate.

Show You Care

We have seen many distressed marriages changed to happy ones when one mate recognized the job pressure of the other and cooperated to lessen it. Complete corrections usually cannot be made quickly. But by showing an interest and working together to diminish work stress you can bring about some relief, which then gives hope that the marriage as well as the job situation eventually will get better.

One difficulty in helping mates with job tension is that sometimes they don't want help. They may even push you away. What then? Practice listening and empathizing. Look for little ways to show interest without forcing yourself on your mate. Make sure your spouse feels free to discuss job problems with you and never act too busy or disinterested. Yes, you may have work problems of your own, but a healthy marriage requires that you have regard for your mate's job as well. As you show genuine concern, your spouse may begin to accept your care.

Suggestions for Change

While some mates may need to be encouraged to slow down in their job commitments, others could use encouragement to "Go for it!" Certainly there are no pat answers about work since each couple's situation is different and varies from one season of life to the next. However, if your mate wants out of your marriage and part of the problem is work-related, the following suggestions may help.

First, if too much work is the problem consider *downsizing*. This means cutting back or scaling down your lifestyle. In our society, we sometimes confuse wants with needs. Perhaps you should reevaluate your "needs" to coincide with a saner work schedule.

Occasionally families downsize by having both mates cut back on their work hours. Others decide that one partner will stay home and manage the family. Children who don't have all the newest clothes or toys won't grow up remembering all their parents *didn't* provide. But if mom and dad split up, they'll not only remember it but suffer damage that will affect them the rest of their lives.[1]

To help the person under job pressure, the family can pitch in to do the household tasks. Junior and Susy can mow the lawn and keep the car clean. They both can learn to help with the cleaning, cooking, and laundry. Children also can be enlisted to help make the home a refuge. Parents need an environment of peace and restoration when they come home exhausted. Children need a refuge too, so everyone needs to work together to make home a pleasant place.

Another way to lessen job pressure is to *shift sideways*. Instead of being promoted to a position where the demands are even greater, a person can sometimes make a "lateral" move to a job with less stress but similar pay.

Some people need to make a *complete career change* to decrease their stress. Perhaps they accepted a job that turned out to be a poor fit, or maybe the job itself changed so the skills required no longer match the person's abilities. A complete career shift must be done with a great deal of thought because education, experience, health insurance, and retirement benefits are probably tied up in this particular job. But switching to a totally different line of work may be a lifesaver—and a marriage saver—for some people.

Before making such a drastic decision, however, give serious consideration to getting some professional career counseling. If that is not an option, we recommend Richard Bolles' excellent book *What Color Is Your Parachute?*[2] It helps people identify their abilities and offers guidance for finding employment that matches.

Be a sounding board for your mate; listen while he or she mulls over the situation and give assurance of your support in whatever decision is made.

Often there are no easy answers to job stress, but if your marriage is coming apart because of it you need to find help and activate some changes quickly. A healthy, happy marriage is worth all the effort you exert to reduce work stress.

Chapter 11

Build Your Mate's Self-Esteem

• • •

JIM WAS UNRAVELING, and I didn't know what to do about it. Almost every part of my Christian life was something I had learned from him. Besides being my husband, he was my spiritual role model. He always had been the optimistic one in our relationship. But now this spiritual leader of a large church and the person who had effectively counseled hundreds of people was irritable and depressed himself. He sat around watching TV or staring out the window, asking, "What is the meaning of my life?"

He couldn't remember ever doing anything significant or with the right motive. He questioned his worth in every area. All he could see in himself were faults and weaknesses.

He was grumpy because he was getting older and told me everything in his life was up for reevaluation, including his commitment to our marriage.

I was astounded! I was also scared. How could this be?

Underneath it all, though, I felt a challenge to join myself with God to make a difference in Jim's life.

Realizing I had grown lax in letting him know how highly I valued him, I determined to help him see his strengths and contributions to life. Others admired him and often let him know it by speaking to him after church, sending notes of gratitude, or talking to him during the week. Some of his admirers were young, intelligent, pretty women in our church from the local university. Many of them had come to Christ or were flourishing in their Christian lives because of Jim's ministry. They often told him how much they appreciated him.

Instead of taking Jim for granted, I decided to look at him through the eyes of a twenty-two-year-old and let him know what I saw. From this new perspective I saw many more things to admire than I'd seen before. I told him about those qualities and reminded him of his past accomplishments. I often complimented him on his appearance and thanked him for what he did for our family.

At first he brushed aside my words and wouldn't believe me. He acted as if he didn't want to hear me. But later he told me that all my comments were accumulating inside him. Because I appreciated him and let him know it, he began to move toward accepting himself again and his self-esteem began to thrive once more.

Wasted Possibilities

When we talk about a good self-image or high self-esteem, some people mistake this for arrogance. We've been taught all our lives not to blow our own horns nor to be puffed up with pride. However, having a good sense of our intrinsic worth is not pride. In fact, valuing ourselves is wise stewardship of what God has given us.

Yes, some people seem to have an exaggerated opinion of themselves, but many of these folks actually feel horribly inadequate deep inside. Their proud exterior is merely a coverup for their insecure interior. Self-important people often fear being honest with themselves because they know they are frauds.

People with a low opinion of themselves, on the other hand, are cheating themselves and others. They feel like such lowly peons that they waste their good qualities and abilities by never fully using them.

Their lives are like shriveled seeds that never get planted and therefore never grow and bloom.

Adults with low self-esteem seldom recognize the problem, but their behavior reveals their doubts about themselves. They may be jealous or critical of others; they may be cross with their children and other people; they may talk too much; or to impress others they may spend money they don't have. But worst of all, they may never try anything new for fear of failure; therefore they never develop their skills, and the world misses out on what they might contribute.

Men and women with a healthy self-image are not braggarts; nor are they drudges. They have an accurate assessment of their strengths and weaknesses. They have confidence that they can succeed in most things yet know that if they fail they can learn from it. They know they don't have every ability or talent, but they develop and use the ones they do have.

People with a truly wholesome self-esteem realize that their value does not lie within themselves. They are who they are and possess what they possess because of God's grace.[1] They recognize where they are strong and wise, but they also acknowledge that their strength and wisdom are gifts from God.

The Making of Self-Esteem

Our self-image begins developing at birth—perhaps while we are still in the womb. Among other things, it is affected by whether or not we are

  ♦ Lovingly touched and caressed
  ♦ Given eye contact
  ♦ Talked to
  ♦ Kept safe and warm
  ♦ Fed

As we grow, we sense from all the important people around us whether we are valuable or a bother; whether we can do things well or always mess up; and whether our ideas are worth listening to or better kept to ourselves. In those early years, we gather information about ourselves from how others act toward us. What others think of us forms what we think of ourselves.

Experts used to believe that self-image was entirely developed and fixed by our early twenties. Now, however, we know that self-image is never completely static; it changes with life's seasons and circumstances.

Adults continue to need positive input from the important people in their lives. Subconsciously, we use our friends, family, and coworkers as mirrors to reflect our worth. If we see that we are respected, listened to, and cared for, it is easier to esteem ourselves.

The two of us have known a few dynamic people who were able to see their worth even though they got little or no approval from others. These are unusual folks; most people are not strong enough to have good self-esteem when they are emotionally battered or ignored by people close to them.

Now, About Your Mate

By now you can see how crucial you are to the health of your mate's self-image. In fact, of all the people in the world, you are the most important.

"Wait a minute!" you may say, "My husband is so wrapped up in his career that he doesn't need me. What's important to him is whether or not he's succeeding at work." Or, "My wife only cares about what her friends think of her. They go shopping together, have a weekly Bible study, and talk about everything. If her friends approve of what she wears, thinks, or does, she's happy. She ignores my opinions."

Yes, other people are important to your spouse's self-image, but what the partners feel about each other is a more powerful force. Many marriage partners, however, grow lazy in showing appreciation, and a marriage that is falling apart is pretty strong evidence that at least one mate is no longer building the self-esteem of the other.

This is where you have an important part. As your mate decides whether to leave permanently or to return, your view of your mate's value is crucial. Not only should you appreciate your mate, you should communicate your appreciation.

Perhaps for the moment your mate has found someone whose opinion counts more than yours. However, you have history on your side. Your years of life together, shared joys and sorrows, children, friends, and extended family will count in the long run, and so will your new campaign to build your mate's self-esteem.

What Is There to Praise?

Right now you may think your mate is totally unworthy of any esteem from you. You certainly don't respect your partner's leaving or being involved with someone else, so what good can you say?

Start by thinking of all your mate's abilities and skills. Write them down so you can refer to them again when things get bleak and you have a hard time remembering anything good about your mate. Then list your partner's positive deeds from the past. Finish by noting all your mate's qualities. Qualities are different from abilities and deeds in that they are an inherent part of a person's character. Even if we lose our abilities or can no longer perform certain deeds, we still have attributes that make us worthwhile.

People use their qualities and abilities either negatively or positively. Someone who is aggressive can be abrasive and domineering or a wise administrator. Someone with a sense of humor may use it to cut others down or lift them up. Sometimes our point of view colors whether we think someone's qualities are negative or positive. Forcing ourselves to look at the positive side of our mate's qualities will give us a new appreciation of them.

After you've completed your inventory, jot down some words of appreciation you intend to say to your mate the next time you are together. Vow to carry out your intentions, no matter what else may transpire.

A Builder, Not a Destroyer

Commit yourself to doing and saying everything you can to build your mate's self-image. Don't allow yourself even one "put down." Following are some ideas that have helped us:

Use Words Wisely

When you are tempted to retaliate with spiteful or angry words—don't. Instead, speak soft words of kindness and affirmation. Recall your mate's past goodnesses and use those as a foundation for complimenting him or her.

Thank your mate for any positive thing you think of, past or present. Your spouse may be surprised that you noticed. On the other hand, don't be put off if he or she doesn't react with joy. I was saying all kinds of positive stuff to Jim, but at the time he didn't let me know that he liked it and was secretly storing it away.

Keep *unconditional love* as your key phrase when you speak to or about your mate. Think of God's unreserved love for you when you were no friend of his. Ask him for his power to speak lovingly to your mate.

Try Touching

For too long we've been wary of touching someone because of sexual implications. There are inappropriate ways to touch, of course. But you and your mate have a right to touch each other. God ordains loving touch between a husband and wife, as we know from reading *The Song of Solomon*.

Many scientific studies have shown the value of human touching to give a sense of well-being. Patients in hospitals or convalescent centers thrive when someone touches them regularly and tenderly. Premature babies struggling for life are more apt to survive and do well if they are touched and caressed.

Experiments have shown that customers are more likely to purchase an item when a salesperson touches them appropriately—a momentary touch on the shoulder or back of the hand. Restaurant patrons give better tips to waiters or waitresses who briefly touch them.

The two of us have learned the joy of touching each other. Sometimes it's with sexual motives, but many times it's just to show love and to communicate with each other. Anyway, touching certainly feels good!

Right now, however, your mate may not want to be touched. Don't be adamant about touching an unwilling partner, but look for times when you can tactfully and briefly touch his or her shoulder, hand, or knee.

If your mate allows more touching, do it. The more positive contact you have, the more materials you will have to use in rebuilding your marriage.

Give Respect

Another way to improve your spouse's self-esteem is to show that you value his or her opinions, preferences, and daily decisions. Nothing tears at self-esteem more than to be treated as if one's ideas and interests are unimportant or disgusting.

If you realize you've been disrespectful in the past, you need to make a concentrated effort to look for areas in which to give approval. Showing respect to your spouse is the right thing to do all the time, but now it's absolutely essential.

Respect will boost his or her self-esteem as well as show your mate that you have good motives. As your partner's self-worth increases because of your efforts, his or her bitterness or indifference toward you will likely lessen.

Reveal Your Admiration

Let your mate know what you admire about him or her, not only by your words but by your actions. Look into your mate's eyes when you speak.

If you can't think of anything to admire, remember what first attracted you to your spouse. Let your memories trigger some feelings of admiration.

Do your admiring both privately and publicly. Don't carry on like a love-sick calf in front of others, but let people know you value your mate.

Be Romantic

Sometimes a lack of romance is part of what has driven a mate away. When a mate does not feel accepted physically, his or her self-esteem lowers. So if your partner gives you any clues that it is permissible to show affection, go ahead.

This, of course, brings up the subject of whether or not you should have sexual intercourse. We used to advise, "Certainly, you should. You are the married partner. That's one way of meeting your mate's needs and redeveloping a closeness."

Now, however, we have the AIDS scare. If your mate has been sexually unfaithful to you, having intercourse may be unsafe for your health. "Safe sex" by use of a condom is a misnomer because accidents can happen, so don't put your full trust in a condom.

You and your spouse will have to determine if the risk of AIDS is an issue. Be certain you can trust your mate's words, and don't let the passion of the moment carry you away. AIDS is fatal.

You can, however, find safe ways of expressing affection without the complete act of intercourse. Until you know through a blood test that your mate is free from the AIDS virus or other sexually transmitted diseases, use safe expressions of love such as hugging and caressing.

As you have opportunity, be romantic. Do little things to show that your mate is special to you. For some, a candlelight dinner or flowers is the appropriate expression; for others, it's just being close and attentive. Some mates are pleased with unexpected love notes. Others like flirtatious gestures. You are the one who knows best what would delight your mate.

Whatever you do, do it with the idea of building your mate's self-worth. As your partner feels more valuable to you and to the world, perhaps you will begin to see a healing in your marriage.

Marv was a miserable person. Life had always seemed unfair to him. He was short, and the other kids at school teased him. He wanted to go to college but didn't have the money, so he took a low-paying sales job. He wanted to marry Lana, but she wouldn't look at him. He settled for Dottie instead.

After four kids and ten years of marriage, he began having an affair with Rhonda in another city. He told Dottie he was in that city on business, but much of the time he was actually living with Rhonda.

Dottie found out about Rhonda and did some serious talking with Marv over the next few months. At times he wanted to keep his marriage and end the adulterous relationship with Rhonda. He would promise to break up with her, but he insisted he needed to tell her in person. He'd go to the other city to do so and then not come home for two or three weeks.

Marv's feelings of inadequacy increased every time he said he'd break off the affair and couldn't follow through on it. He felt pulled between the two women. He was disgusted with himself for not being able to make his own decisions and stick to them.

He worried about messing up his family by his coming and going, so he finally announced he was going to stay away. He moved all his things into Rhonda's apartment.

Dottie was crushed, but she was determined to save their marriage. As part of her rebuilding efforts, she saw that Marv needed a better self-image and wisely decided to do what she could to help build his view of himself.

Marv still came by the house regularly to take the kids to a fast food restaurant, the mall, or a movie, so Dottie grabbed those moments to affirm him. She realized she hadn't done much of that in the last few years. Whenever she spoke of him to the kids, she praised and complimented him. She knew they would pass on the essence of her remarks to him.

She sent light-hearted cards and short letters to him at the office to keep him up on family news, making sure she always said something to show she valued his opinions and personhood. At first, he didn't let her know if he even received the letters or read them, but one time when he came for the kids, he mumbled, "I was glad to get your letter this week."

Marv began to step inside the door when he picked up or dropped off the kids. He acted as if he'd like to stay awhile, so one time Dottie invited him to sit down. As they chatted about insignificant matters, she used eye contact to communicate her positive feelings about him. As he stood to go, she gave him a slight pat on the shoulder. He didn't pull away.

After he left the house that evening, Dottie was on cloud nine. They had made progress! But then Marv didn't come around for nearly two weeks. Her spirits sank as she realized he must have felt they were getting too close again. But she mailed him a couple of cards and greeted him warmly when he finally telephoned.

Dottie kept up her crusade of building Marv's self-esteem whenever she had the opportunity. Over the next year, he began to stand straighter and look her in the eye when they talked. He walked with a more self-confident air. He again spent time visiting with her when he came to the house and began to return her little love pats on the knee or shoulder.

Then Marv told her that he had moved away from Rhonda and was living in his own apartment. He had also applied for a better job and got it. A short time later he told Dottie that he felt good when he talked to her and wondered if they could spend an evening together. Dottie complimented Marv on his new job; by then she found it easy to affirm him.

After three more months they decided to try again to make their marriage work. They went to a church-sponsored seminar that helped them better express their true feelings to each other. They decided they needed to see a marriage counselor to help them with long-standing problems.

After several more months Dottie and Marv were cautiously announcing, "Our marriage is on the road to healing!"

Marv credits Dottie for believing in him when he saw no good in himself. "She just kept hanging on, letting me know I was worth hanging onto," he says.

Maintain "Externals"

• • •

BERNIE LOOKED OUT from his dingy apartment window over the irregular line of dilapidated rooftops. Utility lines sagged from one pole to the next, cluttering most of his view. Even the nondescript birds perched on the wires looked dismal. The dented, overflowing trash cans in the alley below didn't add any beauty to the scene either.

There was only one bright spot—the big, red K on a K-Mart sign. If Bernie stood close to the window and craned his neck to the right, he could see the gaudy sign over the rooftops. If he looked to the left, all he saw were the grimy bricks of another taller building.

This certainly isn't like home, Bernie thought as he envisioned the modest, but well-kept suburban home he and Linda had bought so proudly eleven years ago.

If he were looking out their bedroom window, he would be seeing their sparkling, green lawn with the kids' swing set and sandbox to the right and the picnic table under the pine tree to the left. The yard sloped down toward a line of trees at the back which nearly blocked the neighbor's houses from view. The side fences could use a new coat of stain, but they weren't bad yet. Linda's iris along the left fence would be blooming soon. The backyard had been a happy place, but the memory of it now pricked Bernie like a thorn. What a mess their marriage had become. He thought about what had gone wrong.

It all started when he took on a special project at work. It had meant more income, but it cost him hours away from his family. Before long he hardly had time to turn around at home before he had to go back to the office. Linda showed that she could manage the family without him, but she was becoming like a stranger to him. And he didn't like missing out on everything Mark and Timmy were doing.

Then he became involved with Dawn, a typist at work. When she rolled her big brown eyes at him, Bernie tingled all over. He began taking her to lunch and eventually he asked her to stay after hours to help him. He enjoyed being around this pretty young woman. The night he took her home to her apartment after dinner had been his downfall. They ended up in bed.

Dawn begged him to stay overnight, but suddenly he was sick of her and he sheepishly went home to Linda.

Bernie felt so ashamed that he woke Linda and confessed everything. He told her how sorry he was, but Linda was enraged. She didn't yell because she didn't want to waken the boys, but she was seething. He had deceived her into believing he was working late by himself, and she let him know how hurt and betrayed she felt. The rest of the night, she gritted her teeth and muttered, "How could you do this to me? How could you destroy our family?"

When morning came, Linda demanded that Bernie get out.

"Where do I go?" he asked.

"I don't care!" she retorted. "Rent a motel room or whatever, just get out of my sight!"

Bernie tried to talk to Linda during the next couple days, but she hung up on him whenever he called. One afternoon he went to the house when he knew the boys would be at school. She let him in, and he apologized again.

Linda smiled weakly and said, "I'd like for things to work out for us again. But, I don't know . . . we have a big problem."

Bernie declared that he was no longer seeing Dawn; in fact, he was going out of his way to avoid her at work.

Linda wasn't sure she could believe him, and she sent him away without forgiving him and without resolving anything. But she did make it clear that she didn't want Bernie back home yet. She felt a deep resentment toward him and thought he needed to pay for his failure.

Bernie decided to rent an apartment rather than live in a motel. He couldn't afford much because the family's monthly expenses ate up most of his paycheck. So here he was on a Saturday morning in a dumpy, run-down, cramped apartment. Linda had told the boys that Daddy was sick and had gone away to get better, so he couldn't even go to see them. He had work to do, but he didn't feel like doing it in these surroundings.

He was still stinging over Linda's announcement that he was to get a separate checking account. She was closing out their joint account and getting one with only her name on it because she didn't want his name on the checks with hers. The news made him afraid that she was also closing out their marriage.

When he stopped by the house another time, he noticed she wasn't wearing her wedding ring. He hoped she had it off because she was housecleaning.

Bernie was so discouraged over his isolation from his family that he just stayed around his apartment, letting his loneliness gnaw away at him. Then he made up his mind that he had to get out and be with people. But where? He couldn't go to any church meetings because Linda had him blackballed there.

He began spending more time at coffee breaks with the other employees. Previously, he would take a cup of coffee and drink it at his desk while he worked. Now he longed to chat.

He noticed an attractive woman about his age and began having conversations with her. He found out Ellie was divorced. She was also intelligent and fun to be around. He enjoyed taking her to dinner—even though he would rather have been home with Linda and the boys.

Then the big shock came. A coworker showed Bernie a Christmas card he had received from Linda. It contained a snapshot of the boys with their dog, but the card was signed only "Linda, Mark, and Timmy." Linda really was cutting him out of her life!

He called her and asked the meaning of the Christmas card. "Does this mean you want a divorce?" he demanded. "If you do, say so."

"Of course I don't want a divorce. Some day I'll be ready for you to come home." But inside she was still punishing Bernie.

Bernie was truly confused. If she wanted him, why was she sending so many signals that he was no longer part of her life?

Time went by and Bernie continued seeing Ellie—just for companionship. He called Linda often, but she was always cool to him.

Then one day Linda called him for the first time. She said that she was ready for him to come home and that he could return anytime.

Bernie was bewildered again. For nearly ten months she had shut him out, telling everyone they were separated because of his affair. Now she was waving him back in and he wasn't sure *he* was ready. He had grown fond of Ellie, and going home would mean breaking ties with her.

How could he ever take up a normal life at home? By now his boys thought he had abandoned them because he hadn't been allowed to see them. His neighbors and church friends all knew he had been gone and why. All the people on their Christmas card list assumed the marriage was over. He wasn't sure Linda had forgiven him, and he was afraid she'd hold his failure over his head like a club. Perhaps too many hurdles blocked the way between him and home.

Don't Burn Your Bridges

Many spouses, like Linda, change routines while their mate is away. This causes the partner to feel all the more estranged.

No harm is done by keeping up appearances while your mate is deciding whether or not to return. You aren't being a phony; you're simply making it easier for your mate to come home.

Leave your mate's belongings in place. Don't do as one man did: he gave all his wife's clothing to Good Will after she had been gone only a month. She hadn't taken everything with her because she felt she might return. But he was angry, and getting rid of her clothes was his way of retaliating.

Keep wearing your wedding ring. Don't change the locks on the doors. Keep your mate's name on the checking account unless you have some reason to think he or she will abscond with the funds. Don't tell a lot of people that your mate is gone. Make it as simple as possible for your mate to come back.

Include Your Mate

Keep your mate in the family as much as you can. Invite him or her to traditional family gatherings. Doing so may create an awkward situation for you, but that is better than the chilly isolation your mate might feel from being excluded. Banishment only pushes your mate toward intimacy with someone else.

Keep your spouse posted as to what the children are doing and try to involve your mate in their activities. Say nothing to your children to turn them against your mate, even though you may feel justified in doing so.

If your children question what is happening, give them a simple, honest answer in line with their ability to understand. For example, "Daddy and I are having some trouble right now, but we hope it will get better soon."

If they are angry because of the separation, help them work through their anger without tearing down your mate's dignity. Assure your children that your spouse will always be their parent. Discourage your children from taking sides.

If your mate feels he or she hasn't been ripped out of the family picture, it will make coming home easier. And that's what you're working toward.

Don't Muddy the Water

Rachel had been writing to us for help for about six months. Her husband had left and was living with another woman. Rachel and Bud talked often and sometimes even "dated." She had strong hopes that he would come back home although he hadn't done so yet.

Then we got a letter from Rachel saying:

> I think I'm going to start dating. I still believe that Bud is going to return before the end of the year, but I am so dreadfully lonely while I wait. Wherever I go, I'm like a fish out of water—I'm not divorced, but neither do I seem married.
>
> I don't drink, but lately I've been going to a bar with my girlfriends after work and just sipping a soft drink while we talk. Then sometimes we go eat and see a movie. Lately we've been meeting up with the same three guys at the bar, and they join us for the evening. One of them has taken an interest in me and has asked me out.
>
> Do you think it would be all right to accept? It wouldn't be anything more than a friendship, and it would give me something to do while I wait for Bud to get ready to come home.

Our advice to Rachel was, "Don't do it."

We understand how lonesome a person is while the mate is gone, especially knowing that he or she is with someone else. But if your goal is to make it easy for your spouse to return, you don't want a fourth party scrambled into the mixture—for several reasons.

First of all, you may have trouble keeping your emotions in check. Before you know it, you could become too enmeshed with the other person to make an easy break if your mate decides to come back.

A worse danger is that your mate will learn of your social life and will see it as verification that your marriage isn't working. Since your spouse is probably looking for excuses to justify his or her own unfaithfulness, you would be adding fuel to the fire.

We suggest you meet your needs for companionship by cultivating a few good friends of your own sex. If you are with mixed groups, be in an environment that doesn't lead to pairing up.

This is a tough time, but God is on your side. As you do everything possible to maintain the shape of your marriage, your mate will more likely see that he or she still has a place in it. And you will be glad you did all you could to "maintain the externals."

Chapter 13

Confront Sparingly and Practice Patience

◆ ◆ ◆

A PETITE, DARK-HAIRED woman was waiting for us at the back of the room after we finished speaking at a mid-life crisis seminar. She was attractively dressed and gave us a warm smile. When she introduced herself, we recognized her name from letters she had written to us. Jan looked almost too young to be at a mid-life meeting, but she clearly knew her mission:

"I just had to come see you when I learned you were going to be in my area. Your letters and materials have been a big help to me since my husband left, and I really thank you for them. But now I think it's time I take some action."

"What kind of action?" one of us asked.

"It's been three-and-a-half months since Roger walked out. I've tried all the things you've suggested, but he hasn't changed. You said to try to meet his needs, but how can I? His only need seems to be the other woman," she said firmly.

"Three-and-a-half months seems long now, but . . ." Jim started to say.

Jan interrupted, "That's long enough for him to change his mind, and he hasn't. We're getting together to talk this weekend, and I'm going to confront him. I've been nice long enough, and that isn't working. I think giving him some ultimatums will help."

Jan wanted us to endorse her actions against Roger. Instead we tried to calm her down and discourage her from pressuring him into making an immediate decision. We explained that many people work for months and years to restore their marriage. The ones who win are very glad they were patient. The ones who lose are still glad they didn't hurry into a divorce. They at least have the satisfaction of knowing they didn't give up too quickly.

"Why should I have to go through all that?" Jan asked. "I'll go a little easy on him when I talk to him, but he has to make up his mind one way or the other."

Two months later we heard from Jan. "I should have listened to you," she wrote. "I demanded that Roger either choose me or the other woman. He chose her. He hasn't contacted me since. Now what do I do? I really love him and don't want to lose him."

Ultimatums Get the Wrong Results

When people are pushed against a wall to make a hasty decision, they often choose the opposite of what the mate hopes. Had they been given time to think things through, to let God do his work, and for natural processes to take their course, the decision might have been in favor of the spouse.

Sometimes the best way for confused mates to come to their senses is for them to be on the other side of the fence long enough to learn for themselves that it isn't greener over there, after all. If others tell them that it isn't, they don't believe it; and if someone *demands* that they get back on the right side of the fence, they balk like stubborn donkeys.

Ultimatums cause mates to build barriers to protect themselves from the ultimatum-giver. Undecided mates already feel vulnerable, and when someone starts lobbing boulders at them, they erect a higher wall.

Some uncertain mates don't even stay around to build walls; they just run. And giving an ultimatum to a person on the run is like digging spurs into the side of a horse; it'll make him go faster, but it won't make him change directions.

Patience Is a Virtue

Days and weeks do drag on while you're waiting for your mate to want to be with you again. Each new incident rips at your heart and tries your patience even more. "I just learned he's taking her to Hawaii." "She's let a guy move in with her now." Patience is probably one of the hardest principles to carry out.

We live in a "hurry" society. We get immediate resolutions to problems in TV stories. Commercials promise instant relief from colds, stomach distress, and weight gain. Men and women even compete with each other over whose hair product takes less time to get the gray out.

We microwave our meals and gobble them down in less than ten minutes. We dash and zoom and don't have time to listen to anyone who utters a single "uh-h-h" when speaking.

But some things can't be rushed; they just take time. Restoring a marriage is one of those things that won't happen overnight. When people tell you that your mate is never coming back and that you might as well get on with your life, tell yourself that you can wait. God sometimes works miracles in a flash, but more often he chooses the "process" method—and with good reason. Changes that unfold in stages usually are more permanent than those made hastily.

Patience Requires All Your Resources

Each morning—and many times through the day—you'll have to murmur, "Patience. Patience. God, please give me patience." Perhaps you should even memorize James 1:2–4:

> Is your life full of difficulties and temptations? Then be happy, for when the way is rough, your patience has a chance to grow. So let it grow, and don't try to squirm

out of your problems. For when your patience is finally
in full bloom, then you will be ready for anything, strong
in character, full and complete (TLB).

Besides reading Scripture and praying for patience, keeping yourself busy will help the time go faster. Plan activities with friends or family. Take a class. Learn a new skill. Visit the elderly. It's usually better to do things with other people than to be alone. Doing something *for* someone else will also help reduce the intensity of your problem.

Enlist your friends who know about your situation to pray for you. We've seen amazing turn-arounds in marriages that seemed beyond rescuing. But someone was praying and the impossible happened.

Tina called our home one evening. She was crying and pleading desperately, "Please, please, pray for me and Jack. You know he has been threatening to leave. Well, at this very moment he's with another woman asking her to leave with him. Betty, Jack's secretary, just called to tell me. She happened to step into Jack's office and overheard part of their conversation."

Jack and Tina had been struggling for several months, and now it really looked as if their marriage might not make it.

We prayed with Tina on the phone, and then we prayed some more as soon as she hung up. We begged God to keep Jack from making a mistake. We asked him to do an extraordinary work in both Jack and Tina. We poured out our hearts for several minutes and then we committed Jack and Tina into God's hands. Several of their other friends were praying for them that night as well. So a whole band of folks was imploring God for his intervention during those hours.

The next morning we learned that Jack had not left with the other woman. He had gone home and talked briefly to Tina about his confused feelings before going to sleep. Their troubles were far from resolved, but the crisis had reached a climax. From then on, Tina and Jack cautiously worked to strengthen their marriage. Today they are still together with a much better marriage.

Patience Allows Time for Growth

If you have been taking giant strides in personal growth during your separation, your spouse needs a chance to catch up. If there's too big a gap between the two of you, your marriage could still break. Be patient and give your mate time to blossom.

When you find yourself fretting that this terrifying season is never going to end and you feel like demanding a decision, remember that forcing something to bloom before its time will kill it.

Our four-year-old granddaughter was with us one evening when we were given some long-stem roses. The flowers hadn't opened yet and were only beautiful red buds. We carried them around for a few hours, so they were looking rather droopy when we got to the house. Jim ran water in the bathtub and laid the roses in the water to soak up moisture before putting them in a vase.

After a few minutes I found our granddaughter standing beside the tub with one of the flowers in her hand. She was peeling back the layers of the bud.

"Oh, no, Honey," I said, "you're hurting the flower."

"But I want to see the whole flower," she explained.

Needless to say, that rose never blossomed because it was forced open before its time.

Instead of trying to force God's process of making your marriage blossom again, you can be patient because you have hope—hope in God's plan for you and your mate. You can also be patient because you want to meet your spouse's needs—and one of the needs is not to be pushed.

Keeping Silent about Sin?

Is all this patience simply an endorsement of sin? Are we just making it easier for people to keep committing adultery or to defect from their families?

Some people would argue that we are. They say we should attack the issue straight on. "Tell people to repent or you'll wash your hands of them!" they would advise.

We need to look at the example of Jesus. He, too, "hit the issue straight on." But his blunt and harsh words were directed to the hypocritical religious folks—the phonies putting on a spirituality show. Jesus, on the other hand, was very kind to adulteresses, tax cheaters, alcohol abusers, and people whose tempers got them into trouble. He got to the root of their problem, but he preserved their dignity while he did it. And he brought about permanent change.

Certain people believe we must confront sin with indignation and anger. We have found, however, that hostility will never bring a person to repentance. Even if you manage not to be antagonistic, if you are the slightest bit condescending or give any impression that you feel superior you will alienate the one you're trying to win.

A woman once told us that God had given her the gift of confrontation. As we watched her relate to people, however, we weren't so sure the gift was from God. It seemed more likely that she had an ax to grind and was grinding it on whomever got in her way.

We need to be very careful in challenging people about their sins. Too often the confronting is done more to satisfy the confronter's feelings of self-righteousness and need for power than out of genuine love for the other person.

Useful Confrontation

There will come a time when it is appropriate to speak to your spouse about your side of the situation, but only *after* you have carefully attempted to meet your mate's needs. Confrontation should come after much prayer for wisdom to say the right things and for love to say them kindly.

Be very sure God is telling you it's the right time. Sometimes we convince ourselves God is giving us a message when instead it's our own human nature urging us on. We confuse the Holy Spirit's direction with our human emotions. Timing is very crucial so that your good purposes will not be aborted.

As with any communication, your confrontation should be done quietly and courteously. Make sure your face has a pleasant expression when you use eye contact. Don't put your mate down or try to make him or her feel guilty. State your point simply. Then give your mate time to respond and ask questions.

Your mate needs to know that you want to restore your marriage. Tell your spouse you're sorry for your part in the deterioration and that you want to work on solutions. You want to understand what he or she needs and you'll try to meet as many of those needs as possible.

Don't be surprised if your spouse says it's too late or that he or she no longer has feelings for you. Words like that are often used to test the earnesty of your intentions. Your mate is probably still confused about what he or she wants; so, for now, the response may be cool or even angry. Remember to keep having hope beyond the wall your mate is holding up right now.

Putting It All Together

You are being asked to do some of the hardest things of your life. The natural response is to get angry, give up hope, or whine. But you need supernatural responses and actions if you're going to rebuild your collapsed marriage.

You need strength, patience, and love beyond your own supply as you work to meet your spouse's needs—needs that may take keen detective work to discover now that your mate wants out.

Remember, God stands ready to give you all the supernatural love and persistence you need. Each day, take a fresh grip on God's grace for you.

Chapter 14

Flex, Change, and Grow

◆ ◆ ◆

CAROLYN CAME HOME from her job at the school cafeteria to find a note from her husband:

> I've gone away for a few days. I don't know when or if
> I'll be back. Don't try to find me. Here are some signed
> checks so you can pay the most pressing bills. Tell Rick
> I'm sorry to miss his wrestling tournament.
>
> Take care,
> Wes

Carolyn ran to the garage. Wes's pickup was gone. Then she went to the bedroom closet. Most of his clothes were still there, but he had taken enough to last several days.

Where could he have gone? What could he be doing? Why did he leave without saying goodbye?

She knew he had been nervous and agitated the last few months, and they had quarreled more often than usual. When she tried to show affection he had gruffly pushed her away, saying he wasn't in the mood.

She thought he'd be better once he sold the cattle. He got tense every year when he was watching market prices and trying to decide on the best time to sell his herd. But when Wes sold the cattle this year he made very little profit, so he remained discouraged and irritable. He complained about everything Carolyn did or didn't do. She couldn't seem to do anything right, and she was beginning to not care.

Wes did relate positively to their seventeen-year-old son, Rick, however. Wes was proud of Rick's wrestling abilities and went to all his meets, both home and away. Carolyn detested the smelly gymnasiums and the competitive atmosphere of the parents. She told Wes, "You like that stuff because you haven't really grown up yet." So Carolyn didn't go to the meets, and Wes drove alone while Rick rode with his team.

Now Carolyn wished Wes were around to invite her to the wrestling tournament! This time she'd say yes. She would put up with the miserable surroundings just to be with him.

Her heart was wrenching. She didn't think she could stand this agony of not knowing where Wes was and what was going through his mind. She missed him terribly. She began to think of all the things they had enjoyed together.

Carolyn winced as she realized how little she had done to try to build a good marriage. But she'd been so busy, how could she do more? She worked almost fulltime at the school and still did all the housework. She went to church at least twice a week, and she liked to attend the monthly women's agricultural extension meetings. Besides, she rationalized, Wes didn't do all that much for their marriage either.

Rick came home from the wrestling tournament a little bruised, but more discouraged than hurt. He had only taken third place in his weight class although he'd been expected to get first.

I just couldn't concentrate," he explained. Then he went off to bed without saying much more.

The next morning Rick added a few details to his story about the wrestling match. "I saw Dad last night," he said. "He came to the tournament after all." Rick hesitated and looked uncomfortable before he continued. "I think he had that woman, Trudy, with him. She didn't come with Dad to see me afterward, but I saw her sitting with him during all the events. And she was hanging around the back while Dad talked to me."

Rick banged the table with his fist, let out an expletive he didn't usually let his mother hear, and stormed out of the house, slamming the door behind him. He drove away in his old truck and didn't come back all day.

Carolyn was left alone, shivering and crying. Her hand shook so much that she had to set down her coffee cup. Then her crying turned to wailing. She made so much noise that the dogs outside began to howl. But what did it matter? She was utterly alone.

She didn't go to church that day. How could she face everyone without Wes and Rick? She didn't want to have to explain their absence. Besides, she would just sob all through the service anyway.

Carolyn had heard about us from a friend at church, so the next morning she called our office. Our assistant carefully listened to her and then suggested that our book *Your Husband's Mid-Life Crisis* might be of help.[1] She prayed with her over the telephone, promised to send her some other materials, and invited her to write.

We corresponded with Carolyn for several months, and reading her letters was like watching a cocoon turn into a butterfly. Carolyn went from being a dull, rather self-absorbed woman to a much more sparkling, appealing person. In a matter of days she had made a list of things she needed to do to win her husband back. Instead of moping around the house in the evenings, she attended an oil painting class at the community college. This was something she had always wanted to do but was afraid to try.

Carolyn even decided to attend Rick's last tournament of the season. She asked him to explain some of the rules and techniques so she would know more about what was going on. She put on her most attractive blouse and pants and got out her leather jacket to wear instead of her hooded carcoat.

Wes and Trudy were sitting together on a bleacher when she arrived at the tournament, but Trudy left a few minutes later and didn't come back. Carolyn felt miserable sitting alone, but she had made up her mind to enjoy watching Rick. Finally she got involved in the match, and her excitement and enthusiasm poured out.

After the tournament, Wes walked over. "Hello, Carolyn," he said. "You seemed to enjoy the match." He hesitated a bit and then said, "I was wondering if I could come to the house some night this week. If you want to, we can go eat somewhere." They agreed on a night and each went their separate ways. Carolyn wondered if Trudy was waiting for Wes somewhere.

She decided to put that question out of her mind and concentrate on planning the evening with Wes. She would fix his favorite meal. He'd like that better than eating out. She'd wear the sweater he liked. She wished her jeans fit better, but they'd have to do for now. She vowed to start losing weight so her clothes would look better.

The evening Wes came to dinner turned out better than Carolyn had dared to hope—even though she had prayed for a miracle. Rick ate with them, and it seemed like old times—before the quarreling had begun. They didn't get into any deep, meaningful conversation, but neither did they argue.

Carolyn could tell Wes was watching her every move. He carefully measured each word he spoke, and so did she. She wanted to let him see that she was growing, but she didn't want to tell him outright.

Before Wes left, he said, "Well, you probably wonder when I'm coming home."

Carolyn answered gently. "I think you probably have things you're working out. You'll be home when you're ready. We'll be very glad to have you whenever that is."

Wes seemed relieved by her answer.

"Are you planning to go to the national livestock show in Denver next month?" she asked.

When he said yes, she asked if she could go with him.

He blinked his eyes a moment and then said, "Livestock show? You hate those things."

"I used to, but I'm learning to enjoy things like that. I'd really like to go. I even have a new western shirt I'd like to wear," she said.

"Well, O.K. Sure you can go. I've never liked going by myself," Wes said, surprise still in his voice.

By the time they went to Denver, Carolyn had lost six pounds. Already her pants fit better. She felt peppier and a little like a teenager as she got into the pickup with Wes. They chatted about several family matters on the way. Carolyn even got up nerve to tell him she was taking the oil painting class.

He laughed just like she thought he would. "Oil painting? Isn't that a little classy for a rancher's wife?" he joked.

So, he still thinks of me as his wife, she thought. *That's good!*

At Carol's suggestion, they stayed in separate motel rooms in Denver. She didn't want Wes to feel as if she were smothering him.

When they got home, Wes came to the house more often. They had some good talks about changes they both needed to make if their marriage was going to work. After a few weeks, Wes told Carolyn that Trudy was no longer a part of his life. He still wasn't ready to come home, however, and Carolyn didn't push.

One week she invited him to a special dinner for his birthday. She groaned when she recalled that last year she had been too busy and tired to do anything for his birthday.

After they ate, Carolyn gave Wes a gift. He tore off the wrapping paper to find an oil painting of a Hereford cow under a tree in their pasture. The old windmill was part of the background.

"Wow! This is really good," Wes exclaimed. After studying the painting a minute, he said, "The best place I know for this is over my desk in the den." He immediately went to put it up.

Before leaving, he took Carolyn's hands in his. "I'd really like to move back home, if you'd have me," he said.

"I'd be glad to have you back if you're ready," she said carefully.

They talked a little more and decided he would move home on

Saturday. He gave her a peck on the cheek and walked to his pickup whistling.

Know Yourself

Right now your mate wants out or wants someone else. What you want is for your mate to want you. So part of what's still to be done is some personal work on yourself.

We've never met a married person who didn't need to keep adapting and growing. That's what makes a healthy marriage. Since yours is rather sick right now and you want to bring it back to health, you'll need to take a look at yourself.

If you're ready to admit that some changes in yourself might help your mate see your marriage more positively, hurray for you! Even if your marriage doesn't improve, you'll like the new you.

Before you undertake your self-improvement program, spend some time prayerfully taking an inventory of who you are and what changes you need to make. Jot down what kind of person you are—your personality characteristics, abilities, qualifications, and experience. Make another list of things you like to do or wish you could do.

Keep your lists where you can add to them during the days to come. When you are satisfied that your lists are complete, take your notes and mark the items that are pleasing to your spouse. Then list the things you know your spouse would like you to modify. After considering both lists, decide which areas to start developing and which ones to start changing. Choose those that will make the most difference to your spouse but won't violate your values and personal integrity.

Review Wes and Carolyn

Carolyn found out that she could learn to like wrestling matches and livestock shows without violating her convictions. She also knew that Wes would like her to be thinner—and she'd like to be also. So she went to work on losing weight. She changed some of her wardrobe so she no longer looked old enough to be Wes's mother.

Carolyn also very wisely started growing in a new dimension by taking the painting class. She found personal fulfillment from this and it made her a more interesting woman.

What convinced Wes that Carolyn intended to change was the attention she started giving him. He knew it took extra work for her to cook special meals for him, and he appreciated her effort to become involved in his interests. The painting of the cow was the first time she had ever *made* a gift for him.

He enjoyed having her focus on him. He felt special to her, and it made him want to do something special for her in return. When she spoke gently to Wes it helped him speak more kindly. He liked not fighting. He didn't feel like such a louse or that he was being treated like a little boy.

As he felt better about Carolyn, he also felt better about himself. Carolyn's growth started Wes on a journey of growth, and then he was ready to come home. And he was able to say, "I'm sorry for the pain I caused you by not being open with you and by being with Trudy."

Where There's Life There's Hope

Often we get into a rut in the way we relate to our mates. We forget that our relationship is a living entity, and living things need to grow to stay alive. Some couples fall asleep after the wedding ceremony and ignore the cultivating, fertilizing, and watering necessary for a thriving marriage.

We now live in California where—much to our delight—plants grow and bloom all year. However, California is very dry. It doesn't rain for months, so we must be sure to water our plants frequently. Because they have no dormant period, they also need fertilizer. And, of course, the weeds and pests have to be controlled.

We have a variety of plants and bushes on all sides of our house. One plant we've been enjoying the past several years is a robust geranium in a large pot that we can see from our kitchen and dining room windows. It is more than three feet in diameter and has bright pink blossoms all year long.

Sadly, it's not so healthy now. When Jim was away for a week of college lectures, I was sick and forgot to water the outdoor plants. By the time I remembered, the poor geranium was turning brown.

It kept getting browner until only about one-sixth of the plant was alive. Recently Jim cut away all the dead parts, leaving only a small green plant in the pot. It doesn't even have blossoms. He fertilized it and is watering it faithfully.

Even though only a little bit of the plant is left, it *is alive*. With proper care, it will again grow and bloom. We expect to see a much prettier plant in that pot in a few months.

As you tend your marriage and nurse it back to health, remember to consistently feed, water, and till it. And don't forget to prune the parts that irritate your mate or are dull and boring. You may have only a little sprig of life left now, but *it is life* and can grow into something beautiful again.

Part 3

MEET YOUR
NEEDS

Chapter ♦ 15

Know Your Boundaries

• • •

TED TWISTED HIS wedding ring around and around on his finger. *Should I leave it on or take it off?* he wondered. The rock and roll music blaring over the speakers in the smoky cafe made it hard to think. He picked up his coffee cup, then set it down again on the greasy table top. He continued to turn his ring on his finger.

Melody had made it clear that she was ready to take off her wedding ring if he didn't make good on a few promises and pay more attention to her.

He hadn't bothered to eat breakfast with her that Saturday morning because she was still sleeping and he wanted to get an early start on his day. Before leaving the house, he'd helped Justin find new laces for his basketball shoes. But, no matter what else he was doing, his mind was constantly nagging him to do something to make things better with Melody.

As Ted started to chew his soggy toast, he looked at his watch. Time for him to leave. While he stood at the cash register paying his bill, he worried that he might be making Scott wait. He had told his friend he'd help him take down the dying tree in his backyard that morning.

While Ted and Scott were getting set up to cut the tree, Scott's wife called Ted to the phone. Ted's twelve-year old daughter, Jessica, was crying because he had forgotten to drive her to gymnastics lessons. Melody had already left to go to her part-time job.

"I'll be right there, Sugar," he said.

Ted was embarrassed to tell Scott he had to leave for awhile, but he promised to return as soon as he could.

After he dropped off Jessica at the Y, he saw a little old lady with her grocery carrier piled high. The rickety old cart looked as if it had hauled groceries one too many times; one wheel wouldn't move at all. The frail woman tugged at the cart to make it go and suddenly her tall pile of groceries toppled over.

Ted stopped to help her gather up the groceries. He put them in his car and drove the woman to her apartment. By the time he got her and the groceries inside, it was getting late.

He zoomed back to Scott's house only to find that Scott already had the tree down. He had called on a neighbor to help him. Ted pitched in to make up for lost time.

As he sawed the trunk into short pieces to be split for firewood, he realized he was half an hour late to pick up Jessica. He mumbled his apologies to Scott again and tore off to get her. She was standing near the curb with one hand holding her gym bag and the other on her hips. She scowled as she got into the car and pouted all the way home.

They reached the house as Justin was finishing off leftover pizza. It was an hour after lunch time, so Jessica and Ted each made a sandwich and ate in silence. While they were eating, Justin came into the kitchen carrying a new basketball hoop.

"O.K., Dad, I'm ready for you to help me mount my hoop on the garage," he announced.

Ted looked at the kitchen clock and pressed his temples with his fingers. "Wow, I almost forgot. This is the afternoon Grandma and

Grandpa are expecting you. I told them I'd bring you over about 1:30. It's been so long since they've seen you," explained Ted.

"Oh, Dad, how could you? How could you?" both kids moaned.

Ted decided he'd rather deal with grumbling children than disappointed parents, so with an ugly tension between them, Ted got the kids in the car and headed for his parents' home.

Near the end of the afternoon, Ted drove home with his two kids mad at him for staying too long and his parents annoyed because he didn't stay long enough. He entered the back door to find Melody ready to explode.

"Why isn't the bathroom light installed? It doesn't look like you picked up the drycleaning either. And the garage is as messy as ever. You didn't do one of the things you promised," she stormed.

When Ted tried to explain how he had spent the day, she gritted her teeth and said, "That's it! Everybody comes before me. I don't mean as much to you as a friend with a dead tree. We're finished. It's time for you to get out. Now!"

Out of Bounds

Before Ted got packed, Melody cooled down and asked him not to leave. "But we're going to a marriage counselor!" she declared.

After a couple of counseling appointments, the therapist asked to see Ted for a session alone. During that session the counselor showed Ted that he had a boundary problem. He was trying to please everyone—and wound up pleasing no one.

Ted needed to define himself, to establish priorities for his life and set limitations. He was so busy accommodating others that he was getting trampled and his marriage was being destroyed. He needed to put others in second place and devote time and creativity to make Melody feel special.

Protect What God Has Made

Many of us think we are being Christlike when we let people intrude on us. Even though Jesus poured himself out for people's needs, he rested and he didn't heal everyone. As God he could have; but he was also man, and he stayed within his human limits by touching or speaking healing words to only one or a few at a time.

While we should serve others, we can't help anyone if we exhaust ourselves. It is appropriate to have boundaries. It is not being selfish to recognize and protect the center that is self. Self is a gift God has given us.

A part of God's design for us is inner wholeness, and that includes knowing our value to God and protecting ourselves. We should not allow others to walk all over us. Protecting ourselves is not self-centered; it's good stewardship of God's gift.

We need to clearly know our boundaries in various areas of our lives—emotional, physical, financial, etc. Many of us can remember times we've been taken advantage of in these areas.

Demands on our time are probably the most common exploitations. These impositions can drain us both emotionally and physically. Other boundary violations are inappropriate touching, molestation, or sexual abuse.

Trampled Fences

The first time Bonnie met her boyfriend's father, she felt uncomfortable. He hugged her too closely and held her too long. He made comments about her physical appearance that sounded like a come on.

Oh, well, maybe I'm too much of a prude, she told herself.

Bonnie married her boyfriend, Eric, but was continually alarmed by her father-in-law's inappropriate touching and remarks. Thankfully, he lived halfway across the continent, so they didn't see each other often. Whenever he arrived for a visit, Bonnie would turn her face when he greeted her so his kisses would land on her cheek rather than her lips. But he still pressed his body too close to hers.

Bonnie avoided her father-in-law as much as she could whenever he visited. But he had sneaky ways of walking past her and moving his hands down her sides along her breasts and over her hips and quickly leaving the room before she could protest.

Eric dismissed his father's improper behavior. "That's just the way he is," he'd say. Since her husband downplayed the man's actions, Bonnie decided not to make a scene over the situation and just let each incident slide.

After thirty years, though, Bonnie became aware that her father-in-law's liberties were *totally wrong*. He had no right to touch her the way he did, and she became angry that Eric hadn't protected her all these years. She felt dirty and used.

When her father-in-law visited the next time and again violated her with inappropriate touching, Bonnie felt she had to speak to Eric about it and ask him to help her put a stop to it.

Bonnie knew she risked upsetting Eric and causing trouble in their marriage if she complained about his father, but she decided that she must do it for her own health and recovery. Surprisingly, Eric did not get angry. He admitted that his father was out of bounds, but still he did not act on her behalf.

Bonnie and Eric started seeing a counselor for help in their marriage, and then Eric saw how very wrong his father was. He realized that all his life he had justified his father's offensive sexual behavior as permissible because he was his father.

When the full impact of all that Bonnie had endured hit Eric, he was filled with remorse that he had allowed his father's improper conduct. He tried several times to confront his father about the matter, but his father denied any wrongdoing. Finally, for Bonnie's safety, Eric and Bonnie agreed that she would have no further contact with her father-in-law.

It is right to protect our boundaries, but sometimes we don't realize when our borders are being violated. Nor do we know what to do when we are aware of it. As we become more confident of our value as God's creation, we can more easily recognize boundary abuses. We also will be more self-assured so that we can calmly put a stop to the violations.

Scripture says:

> Don't give holy things to dogs, and don't throw your
> pearls before pigs. Pigs will only trample on them, and
> dogs will turn to attack you (Matthew 7:6 NCV).

The Dilemma

A further question, though, is how can you balance self-protection with meeting your mate's needs? You want to do all the right things to heal your marriage, but how do you do that and not violate yourself?

Much of what we are suggesting to help your mate come back to the marriage does call for sacrifice on your part. But some of the suggestions are simply common courtesies that should have been a part of your relationship anyway—empathy, listening, encouragement, and patience, to name a few.

Balancing your marriage-rebuilding activities along with protecting your boundaries begins with *your own commitment* to save your marriage. You are the one deciding to go the second—or the ninety-second—mile to help your mate. No one else is making you do it.

It is your decision to turn your cheek, and you're doing it with the long-range goal of reclaiming your marriage. You are making the choices to sacrifice; the choices are not being forced upon you. You know who you are and what you want. What you want is a restored, mutually satisfying marriage.

Handling Abuses

While you're working to rebuild a healthy, happy marriage, how much mistreatment should you take from your mate?

If your mate is verbally abusive to you, be calmly assertive as you tell him or her that that kind of talk is neither helpful nor appropriate. If you have to, remove yourself from the verbal onslaught.

You do not need to be a doormat, but it is important to remember that being *assertive* is different from being *aggressive*. Assertiveness is expressing your opinions and observations in a non-violent manner and with confidence that your thoughts and feelings are worth considering. Being aggressive means you are offensive and warlike. You are argumentative and insensitive to the other person's feelings.

If, however, your spouse is being physically abusive, get away at once. We do not advocate unlimited patience while your face is getting smashed. Your goal of restoring your marriage isn't going to be met while you're being pounded black and blue. Protect yourself and get out of there.

Kathy frequently got so angry and frustrated that she yelled and pummeled her husband, Rob. She would become so distraught that she didn't realize what she was doing.

After one beating, Rob calmly said, "Kathy, I love you very much and I'll never divorce you. But I cannot live with you like this. You must get some help."

Kathy found a counselor and during the first session she became aware that she had been sexually molested as a child. Even though she had enjoyed many happy years of growing up and had done well throughout high school and college, this ugly, forgotten boundary violation was slowly poisoning her.

Marriage brought the damage from childhood attacks to the surface. Sexual intimacies began to be nightmares. Even in routine, daily matters, Kathy would become enraged if she thought Rob was taking even a slight advantage of her or getting too much power.

Through counseling, Kathy began the healing process. Rob also went to a therapist for a time, and today their marriage is back on a healthy track. Rob's quiet, but insistent demand that Kathy get professional help was much more effective than if he had retaliated or silently walked out.

You are a valuable person with God-given rights. You deserve respect.[1] You also want to reclaim an important relationship—your marriage. Therefore, use all your energies and abilities to bring about this recovery.

In so doing, you are not denigrating nor defaming yourself. You are engaging in a noble enterprise that adds dignity to you and to your mate.

Chapter 16

Esteem Yourself Too

• • •

OPAL PULLED UP A CHAIR at the conference center dining room table and said, "I'm glad we can have a few minutes together. I have so much to tell you two since I last saw you."

We had met Opal a few years earlier when she looked more like a scared rabbit than a grown woman. She was being physically and verbally beaten by her husband who constantly cut her down for being dumb and worthless. She had a heart of gold, but her husband was trying to pound it out of her. For twenty years he yelled and swore at her, saying she could do nothing right.

Then suddenly he left her and three teenage children, filed for divorce, and was totally gone. This "worthless" woman now had full responsibility for providing for her family. Her income had been a nice supplement to her husband's salary but it was not nearly sufficient to pay all the bills.

Her kids said, "Mom, we'll make it," and they found after-school jobs to help meet expenses. They loved and respected their mother and encouraged her to get more education so she could find a better job.

But I could never study, she told herself. *I'm too stupid to learn anything new.*

Suddenly she realized those words were only menacing echoes from her former husband. Putting his lies out of her mind, she decided to try a few courses in nursing at a community college. She did very well, and with each succeeding semester felt increasingly confident about herself and her abilities. She went on to become a registered nurse.

Because of her caring heart and natural leadership abilities, she soon was made a supervisor in a home for the elderly. She thoroughly loved the work and the people. She even loved herself. Opal glowed as she rehearsed for us what delight she now had in life. She had learned she not only could do some things right, but she was *very* competent and needed.

Your Self-Worth

Right now you may feel like a rotten piece of rubbish, but that is not the truth. You are special, even if your mate doesn't think so. If you remind yourself of your good qualities and strengths you can esteem yourself whether or not anyone else does.

Your self-image has been influenced from birth by the responses you've received from the important people around you, just as we discussed in chapter 11 regarding your mate. If the majority of your life experiences have been happy and successful, your view of yourself is probably positive.

If you have been abused, ridiculed, or ignored, your self-esteem is likely to be poor. Or perhaps something has happened in later life to change your physical appearance or abilities, and, as a result, your self-image has been lowered. Life's tragedies—such as deaths, illnesses, and disappointments—can be so heavy and so numerous that your view of yourself suffers serious damage. Certainly, your mate's negative response to you right now is battering your self-worth.

Although people and events have been important in developing who you are, you can build your own self-esteem. You are not totally dependent on others for your value.

Learn Who You Are

The best place to find out your worth is from Scripture. God values you and wants you to value yourself.

First of all, you're worthwhile because God made you in his image, as recorded in Genesis 1:26. In addition, you are an asset to God. We are assured of this in such passages as Ephesians chapters 1 and 2. The Living Bible edition of the New Testament makes God's purpose and love for us very clear. Ephesians 1:11 and 18 are especially good, telling us that because of what Christ has done for us we are "gifts to God" and "God has been made rich" by us.

You're also needed for God's plan for the world and for the people in it, as expressed in Ephesians 4:16:

> Under his direction the whole body is fitted together perfectly, and *each part in its own special way helps the other parts*, so that the whole body is healthy and growing and full of love (TLB, emphasis ours).

Psalm 139:1–18 is a classic section of Scripture, assuring you of your worth. God knows everything about you and still loves you. He is always with you. He "precedes" and "follows" you and places his hand of blessing on you. Further along the passage tells you that God made "all the delicate, inner parts" of your body and "knit them together in [your] mother's womb." He was there while you were "being formed in utter seclusion." The Creator of the entire universe is thinking about you constantly. That ought to tell you that you're precious!

Evaluate Yourself

As you did when taking inventory of your mate, now make some lists about yourself. We suggest that you make a list for each of the following:

- ◆ Your abilities, skills, education, and experience (list at least twelve items).

- Your qualities and personality characteristics (list at least twelve items).
- All the things you like to do, whether or not you presently are doing them (list at least fifty items).

These three lists should help you make a fourth:

- All the things you would like to accomplish in your lifetime.

As you study these lists, you will get to know more about yourself. Are you a people person? A detail person? An administrator? A support person? An outdoor lover? An artist? A traveler or a homebody? Does solving problems intrigue you or frazzle you?

There are no right or wrong answers. The combination of abilities and preferences that makes up *you* is what's right. Whatever kind of person you are, you can be glad for what God has made!

Don't Run Yourself Down

Self-criticism is a serious disease. When you think poorly of yourself and make insulting remarks about yourself, you are really criticizing God. Do you ever make any of these remarks about yourself?

- "I can't do anything right."
- "I made the same dumb mistake again."
- "I look awful. (I'm too tall, short, fat, thin, bald, poorly dressed. . . .)"
- "I just can't do it—I'll fail again."
- "I can never be as talented as he or she is."
- "I'm not needed."
- "My illness or disability makes me undesirable."

These ideas are counter-productive! The more you feed yourself these thoughts, the more they become part of you.

Start telling yourself the opposite of the above:

- "I can do many things right."
- "I made the same mistake, but this time I'm going to learn from it."

- "I may be too tall (short, fat, thin, bald, or poorly dressed . . .), but inside I'm becoming more beautiful every day."
- "I will try to do it. Please guide me."
- "I may not have his or her talents, but I do have talents that are suited for me."
- "I'm an important part of God's design; someone needs me in some way."
- "My illness or disability may slow me a little, but I'm still necessary in God's blueprint for the world."

Vow to stop knocking yourself. Never, never say negative things about yourself. When the temptation comes, turn it into a positive remark or say nothing.

That commitment goes for the things you say to yourself as well. Put negative thoughts about yourself out of your mind. As you speak positive, godly thoughts about yourself and to yourself, you will begin to live up to them.

Respect Your Physical Body

"Take good care of yourself; you belong to me," are lines from an old popular song. If you understand that you are valuable, you will realize that you deserve good physical treatment.

Your ability to meet your mate's needs will be enhanced as you meet your own needs. You will do a better job of restoring your marriage if you are in good physical shape.

Get Sufficient Sleep

Being rested is important during this time of stress. Some people are too nervous and tense to get a good night's sleep, or they aren't in bed enough hours for sufficient sleep.

This is not the time to skimp on rest. Your perception of your mate and your situation will be hindered if you are tired. Matters may seem worse or bigger than life simply because you're worn out. You may snap at your mate when you don't intend to because your guard is down due to fatigue. Researchers tell us that three days of sleep deprivation can cause bizarre psychotic symptoms.

Consult a doctor if you are not getting enough sleep. It could make all the difference in rebuilding your marriage.

Weighty Problems

Proper weight is important to your physical well-being during this stressful time. If you are too much underweight, you may have a health problem that is not yet discernible to you. Also, if you're too thin, you may not have enough "reserve" for your immune system to fight disease.

Most of us, however, have more trouble with being overweight, which we all know is dangerous. Extra weight contributes to heart disease, makes us less peppy, and may be repulsive to our mate.

Whether your problem is being too thin or too fat, it is important to take care of your weight. You may be under too much stress to add a rigorous weight control plan to your life at this time, but you can start to improve your eating habits.

You Are What You Eat

It is crucial that you get adequate nourishment during this stressful time with your mate. A well-balanced daily diet consists of protein (meat, beans, legumes); dairy products (milk, cheese, yogurt); grains (bread, cereal, pasta); and fruits and vegetables.

For good health, choose more poultry and fish than beef and pork. Avoid rich gravies and sauces. Cut out as much fat as possible. Fat not only adds weight, it also clogs arteries. Lower your sugar and caffeine intake. You can substitute fruits or vegetable and fruit juices for sweets or soft drinks.

It's best to eat at least three small meals a day rather than to skip meals. You need all the vim and vigor you can get while you're under the tension of your threatened marriage. Good eating habits will help you have the emotional and physical strength to cope with a mate who wants out.

Move Those Muscles

Another way to increase your physical heartiness is through exercise. Exercise not only burns calories, it promotes the release of endorphins, which circulate in the blood and relieve tension.

Choose a regular exercise plan that fits your schedule and interests. You may like the stimulation and equipment of a health club, or perhaps you'd rather have exercise equipment in the privacy of your home. You may be a swimmer, biker, or jogger. Pick an exercise that is convenient and enjoyable and you'll be more likely to stick with it. Think of exercise as part of your daily routine, as you do bathing, dressing, and eating. You don't go without those!

We have found walking to be our best exercise. We don't need special equipment except for comfortable walking shoes. We don't have to do it at any specified time. We don't need to drive to another location. We don't have to take a shower afterwards. While losing a little weight, we get to enjoy the birds and flowers, plus we get away from the day's pressures.

We walk at least six times a week. Fortunately, we now live in a climate that accommodates our habit. When we lived where winter and wet weather were a problem, we used an inexpensive exercise bike during bad weather.

The generally accepted rule in exercising is to get your heart rate up to 120 for twenty minutes at least three times a week. Exercise should be done only with your doctor's approval, however, so check with a professional about how strenuously you should work out.

Keeping yourself physically fit will help you to value yourself and better cope with your marital stress.

Enjoy Your Appearance

"Man looks at the outward appearance, but the LORD looks at the heart" (1 Samuel 16:7) is a frequently quoted Scripture verse. Often we emphasize the second part of the verse—that God sees our hearts—and forget the first part.

Since our exterior is what others see, we generally feel better about ourselves if we're pleased with our appearance. Without putting undue importance on clothes, hair, and other externals, keep in mind that you're doing yourself a favor to look as good as you can. You are worth it.

Your mate likely will appreciate it too. In fact, people we know have started to reconsider their desire to break their marriage when they've seen their spouse lose weight, dress better, and get a new hairstyle. Appearance isn't all that makes or breaks a relationship, but it may have more influence than we imagine.

At a college reunion we noticed that the divorced women looked more attractive than the married ones. They were thinner, had hairstyles that were more becoming, and wore up-to-date clothes. Before their marriages broke, the divorced women had looked as mediocre as the others. Apparently they learned after their divorces the importance of a good appearance. Married people would do well to find the key to looking good while still married.

You may not have money to spend on new clothes, so do the best with what you have. Study TV and magazine ads to see what the people of your sex and age are wearing. Then improvise with inexpensive accessories or new combinations from your existing wardrobe. It's better to have a few clothes in style that you wear frequently than to wear a lot of out-of-date clothes that signal you must not know the difference.

Personal hygiene is also important. Clean hair, teeth, nails, and body will make you feel good, and everyone around you will enjoy you more.

You will like yourself better if you do the most with what you have, whether it's your clothes, face, nails, or hair. In many ways you're in competition with whatever force is pulling your mate away from you, so take some steps to be in the running.

Nourish Yourself Emotionally

Sometimes when we're under stress, we try to run on an emotionally empty tank. We're so consumed by our problem that we neglect to refuel our spirits.

Everyone needs to do some little thing that restores them every day, but the type of activity will vary for each person. For you it may be reading, running, taking a bubble bath, playing the piano, spending time on a hobby, working in the yard, or being with a friend. Choose whatever nourishes you and do it regularly. Much of the day depletes your emotional energy, so be sure to do something every day that refuels your spirit.

Part of emotional nourishment is accepting new challenges. Don't get in over your head, but try something different: develop a new sport or hobby, volunteer in a hospital, cultivate a new friend, or even take a different job.

Take time for reflection and meditation. If you're buzzing with activity to the point that you never have any thinking time, you're doing yourself a disservice.

Some of the most important growth the two of us have experienced has come from reading or listening to what others have learned about living successfully. You too can grow through the use of self-help books or tapes.

Nourish yourself emotionally by being with positive friends rather than negative ones. Instead of being dragged down by people who drain your emotions, spend time with the kind who fill you with joy and hope.

Find as many ways as possible to appreciate yourself. Be good to yourself. You aren't being selfish—you're filling your emotional tank so you have something to give to others. You especially need a full tank so you can give to your mate and restore your marriage. Caring for yourself is important to you, your mate, and your family.

Chapter 17

Put Yourself
in God's Hand

• • •

THE SAND BLEW IN the front door, across the living room floor, and joined the dust balls around the unmade bed in the barren three-room apartment where Ted was staying. Sand settled between the pages of a book he had dropped on the floor after reading in bed one night. That didn't matter; it was just another example of the bleakness of Ted's life. A dismal feeling of power-lessness nearly overwhelmed him. He felt desperately lonely and utterly rejected. He was deeply aware of his failure, yet he could do nothing to change the situation. Ted wasn't used to having his back against the wall with no way to turn. He definitely didn't like feeling so helpless.

He was an independent man. He didn't normally need help, but he knew he needed it now or he might go crazy. While searching for some relief from his torment, he remembered the Bible. He used to read it a lot. In the last few years, though, he hadn't even opened the cover. He had made a commitment to Christ as a teenager, but he had almost forgotten about that. He and Connie hadn't been to church in years; they had been faithful in attending until they got busy with their growing family.

Ted and Connie, you may remember from chapter 2, are the couple who divorced and then remarried each other.

Ted went to the house when he knew Connie would be gone and rummaged around until he found the small black Bible he had as a kid. He took it back to his apartment. He found the Psalms and began to read like a starving man at a banquet table. Wow! What great promises were in those verses!

He finished the Psalms in a few evenings and began reading the Gospels. He liked the teachings that assured him of Christ's love for him. He could tell that Christ was a powerful man but also had immense love and tolerance for people.

For the first time in years, he began to hold a prayer conversation with God that was more than "Bless me, my wife, and my kids. Amen." The further he read in Scripture, the closer he felt to God and the more he had to say in prayer.

As he went about his work each day, he talked to God silently. He sensed that he wasn't alone after all. He had a friend with him everywhere he went. Some of his desolation began to lift.

Even though Connie hadn't changed her mind about the divorce, some of the sting was gone because God shared the hurt.

As the months went by Connie began to show interest in getting back together, and Ted prayed all the more fervently. Eventually they worked out their differences and married each other again.

Ted then said to us, "I wouldn't want to have to go through that mess again, but it certainly did bring me back to the Lord. I might have cracked up if I hadn't been able to talk over my troubles with God."

Finding Your Security

"Friendship with God is reserved for those who reverence him. With them alone he shares the secrets of his promises" (Psalm 25:14 TLB).

Throughout Scripture we are guaranteed God's friendship, love, and protection as we turn to him. When we put ourselves in his hand—knowing we have no power[1] nor goodness[2] of our own—he will abundantly supply our needs. Christ, by his death and resurrection, paid for our very lives.[3] In him we have everything we could ever need.

John 10 compares believers to sheep who follow a trusted shepherd. Verse 27 says, "My sheep hear My voice, and I know them, and they follow Me" (NASB). Then we are given this wonderful promise of security with the shepherd and his Father:

> I give eternal life to them, and they shall never perish; and no one shall snatch them out of My hand.
>
> My Father, who has given them to Me, is greater than all; and no one is able to snatch them out of the Father's hand.
>
> I and the Father are one (John 10:28–30 NASB).

We can all place ourselves in this harbor of safety by a simple act of our will. We do this by confessing our unworthiness and accepting his worthiness in exchange.

In His Hand You Are Loved

Many people know John 3:16: "God so loved the world that he gave his only begotten son. . . ."[4] But many of us long to feel God's love more personalized. We want to know that God's compassion is for us as individuals rather than for one gigantic mass of people. The mass includes us, of course, but we are especially encouraged when we see that God knows us as separate persons.

As you search for this intimate love, begin with the plea in Psalm 17:7, "Show me your strong love in wonderful ways, O Savior of all those seeking your help" (TLB). Then watch for all the ways God reveals his love to you. Keep a list of God's kindnesses each day. "See for yourself the way his mercies shower down on all who trust in him" (Psalm 34:8 TLB).

Instead of concentrating on the times you feel ignored or misunderstood, look for the times when you are respected and appreciated. Count the times that things work well for you rather than only the times they don't.

Read the Psalms and underline the verses that speak of God's love and protection. You won't get very far before you'll be amazed at God's many assurances of his faithfulness.

As you read the New Testament, note how much God does for us because of his love for us. We are dearer to him than our own children are to us.[5]

You may or may not have had a tender earthly father, but you probably feel affectionate and protective toward your own children or grandchildren. Think of the person you love the most and realize that God's love far exceeds any earthly love you can feel. And nothing can ever separate us from his love. No person or force in heaven or hell or on earth is strong enough to tear us out of God's hand.[6] His love is forever!

In His Hand You Are Safe

Whether or not you ordinarily are a strong person, you probably feel very vulnerable now. Remember the symbols of safety the Bible uses. God promises we are safe in his hand.[7] He is like a shield to us[8] or a towering rock of safety.[9] We are safe under his wings, like baby chicks sheltered by a mother hen from storms and dangers.[10]

These are only a few of the figures of speech the Bible uses to show God's protection. Not only are we dearly loved, we are also dearly kept. Psalm 46:1–5 promises us that

> God is our refuge and strength, a tested help in times of trouble. And so we need not fear even if the world blows up, and the mountains crumble into the sea. Let the oceans roar and foam; let the mountains tremble!
>
> There is a river of joy flowing through the City of our God—the sacred home of the God above all gods. God himself is living in that City; therefore it stands

unmoved despite the turmoil everywhere. He will not delay his help (TLB).

God is on your side.[11] If God is for you, who can be against you?[12] Circumstances and people around you may be blasting you, but you are safe with the one who knows the best plan for you and has the power to carry it out.[13]

Lettie was shaking badly as she closed the garage door and went into the house. She was tempted to just let herself fall apart—to quit fighting for her marriage. Instead she took a deep breath and murmured a prayer for help as she put the teakettle on to heat.

She had just been out to the logging area to see her husband, Paul. For several weeks they had been having bitter arguments and long periods of cold silence, and for the past several nights he hadn't come home. She had heard he was sleeping at the trailer home of Violet, a woman who frequently took in "troubled" men. Lettie thought perhaps this afternoon she could talk to Paul at work.

She drove deep into the woods before she spotted Paul's truck. She was maneuvering her car to the side of the narrow road to park when she noticed an old pickup pulled off under the trees. As she got out of her car, she called loudly for her husband.

The door of the pickup opened and Paul got out, an embarrassed expression covering his face. Then Lettie saw Violet through the pickup window. Suddenly Lettie was so overcome that all she could do was scream, "Oh, Paul! Paul! Paul!"

Without another word she ran to her car and started back down the narrow road out of the woods. Above the noise of her sobbing, she heard the sound of a truck behind her on the bumpy trail. She looked in her rearview mirror and saw Violet coming in her old pickup.

Lettie could see Violet gripping the steering wheel with both hands, and the determined, angry look on the woman's scowling face scared her. Then Lettie felt the pickup ram the back of her car. It let up a bit and then rammed again even harder.

Lettie couldn't believe it! She was going as fast as she could over the narrow, rutty road. The wall of trees on each side prevented her from turning off to avoid the attacking pickup. Again and again she was rammed from the rear.

When they finally reached the main highway, Violet pulled out around her, violently honking her horn, and roared on down the highway. Lettie was trembling all over. She stopped the car to regain her composure before driving home.

When at last she reached their modest little house on the edge of town, she quickly pulled into the garage and began to sob. As her anguish poured out she felt God's strong arms around her. For some weeks now she had been learning to rely on God for her strength.

As she made herself a cup of tea, the telephone rang. When she picked it up, the person on the other end hung up without a word. In a few minutes, the phone rang again. Lettie let it ring twice before she picked it up. Again someone hung up.

The telephone rang throughout the evening. Sometimes she let it ring without answering it, but then she'd wonder if it were Paul trying to reach her. So the next time she would pick it up, only to be left in silence again.

Lettie was sure it was Violet trying to intimidate her. At first she cried out into the lonely house, "Oh, God, I'm not safe anywhere from that woman!" But then Lettie decided that instead of allowing this matter to rattle her she would turn it over to God. Throughout the evening she repeated to herself part of a Psalm: "You are my hiding place; you will protect me from trouble and surround me with songs of deliverance" (Psalm 32:7).

With that promise running through her mind, she was able to go to bed and sleep in peace. For many months Lettie had to draw on God's special protection and care.

Eventually Paul did come home. But he wouldn't get counseling to work on their problems, so their relationship was still stormy. Lettie knew she would need to stay in God's tender hand.

In His Hand You Are Enabled

We aren't kept in God's hand only to be treasured and preserved. We are also empowered to get moving. God has plans for us to carry out rather than stay cuddled in dormancy. Once we've had our batteries recharged, we can get back to the business of marriage restoration, knowing we can be recharged as many times a day as necessary.

Philippians 2:13 says, "God is working in you to help you want to do what pleases him. Then he gives you the power to do it" (NCV).

We don't have to live by our own fortitude. In fact, if all we have is our own resources, we will soon fail. Our courage and energy will quickly wear thin. But we are promised that we can "do everything through [Christ] who gives [us] strength" (Philippians 4:13).

God's mighty hand enables us to act. In addition, he loves us with a love deeper than any other known love, and he keeps us safe. He doesn't fail. In his hand we are truly protected.

Part 4

TOGETHER
AGAIN AT
LAST. . . .

Chapter ◆ 18

Rebuild Carefully

• • •

A N EXCITING TIME is here! You and your mate have decided
to try again to make your marriage work. You no doubt have
some questions and maybe some misgivings. You wonder if you'll be
successful this time.

We hope you're not thinking, *Now that my mate has given up the
third person, we can get on with life and be happy again.* Or, *Once we are
under the same roof again, everything will be great! Just like the old days.*

Perhaps your mate doesn't want the "old days." Something in
the old marriage caused your mate to want to leave, so you need to
build a *new marriage.* You'll use the same two people, but both will
have to change so you don't fall back into the same old habits that got
you into trouble.

Careful consideration about many issues needs to go into your
decision to get back together. If you reunite without confronting the
problems that caused the collapse of your marriage in the first place, your
relationship may fall apart again, making it less likely to ever be restored.

Include the Architect

You will want the best architect available to help you rebuild your marriage. Therefore, as you put your marriage together again, ask God to reveal exactly what needs to be done.

> If the Lord doesn't build the house, the builders are working for nothing (Psalm 127:1 NCV).

Each couple will have a different set of directions, but the following efforts should go into every marriage restoration project:

Build a Solid Foundation

Your marriage will crumble into ruins within a short time unless you take time to build a strong base. Remember the parable of the wise man who built on solid rock and the foolish man who built on sand.[1] The house on sand collapsed when the storms came, but the house on the rock stood firmly. The following things need to be done to rebuild your marriage on a sturdy foundation:

Deal with Past Problems

Clearing the obstacles that nearly ruined your marriage is perhaps the most difficult part of your rebuilding process. It could be compared to bulldozing the property where you plan to put your foundation.

The tricky part is that earlier bad habits and experiences are like landmines planted in your marriage. You and your mate may still be very tender or defensive about past problems. When you start to discuss them, your whole rebuilding process could blow up in your face. Somehow you and your mate have to defuse those explosives without destroying yourselves in the process.

Don't simply bury your grievances and try to get on with life. That's what you did in the past, and that's why you have landmines now. If you refuse to acknowledge and resolve the old hurts and complaints, you will spread another layer of dirt over the landmines and only delay the inevitable blowup.

Time is necessary to work through the past problems. You can't deal with everything in one marathon talk session. You will need to have many discussions over a period of time.

You may need a marriage counselor. Choose one who is skilled in restoring marriages. A wise counselor can give you insights you don't have. The therapist will probably give you assignments that will help you rid the old wreckage from your lives and get ready to continue building.

Forgive and Move On

Once you have uncovered all the landmines, you can begin to defuse them. And that is done through forgiveness. Forgive as much in little steps as you are able. Sometimes it is impossible to forgive all violations against us in one grand gesture.

Honest forgiveness quite frequently comes in stages.[2] The first stage is to acknowledge that you have been wronged. Granting forgiveness presupposes that an offense has been committed or there would be no reason for forgiveness.

Don't just say, "That's O.K. It was really nothing." It *was* something, and if you acknowledge it you can forgive it. If you deny any wrong occurred when it actually did, you cannot forgive it.

Another part of forgiveness is to grieve the losses that the offenses caused. Don't try to take a shortcut by omitting this stage. That would be like putting a bandaid over a wound that first needs to be opened and drained. Admit that damage has happened and pour your heart out to God about your losses.

You will eventually reach the place where you can grant a sincere "grace forgiveness." "Forgiveness is always unmerited. In the last analysis, no one can ever earn forgiveness. It must be granted as a free gift by the person who has been offended."[3]

What if your mate doesn't regret the wrongdoing? Do you still forgive? Yes, after you've worked through the stages of forgiveness. Many times true apologies from your mate will come later, and often they don't come stated as clearly or in as much detail as you would like. Your mate may feel that he or she is showing repentance simply by coming back to you. To demand an apology stated explicitly in your language may be unrealistic at this point.

Forgiveness is needed on both sides. You know your mate has offended you and needs forgiveness, but you also have offended your mate and need forgiveness. To help clear away the rubble in your relationship, start by asking for your mate's forgiveness. This may elicit apologies from your spouse, but that is not the reason for asking—you're asking because you need it.

Forgiveness is like a giant eraser. Once the old marks are wiped away, you and your mate will be able to start writing a new script on the clean surface.

State Your Expectations

Think through what you want in your new relationship. Both you and your mate should decide what will be important for happiness together. Be very specific. Don't just say, "I'd like harmony." Name what actions and attitudes you need to make you satisfied. For example:

- "I need some wind-down time when I get home from work."
- "I need more help with the housework. Perhaps we could alternate getting groceries and doing laundry."
- "I need my own closet and drawer space."
- "I need to be spoken to in a kinder and calmer tone of voice when something is bothering you."
- "I need to have my opinions respected and my viewpoints considered."
- "I need affection other than when you want sex."

The more clearly you each state your expectations, the fewer unpleasant surprises you'll have later on. Naming expectations also provides a ground rule when certain situations arise.

For instance, you may be ready to tromp all over your mate because you're upset about something. Then you remember your spouse requested that you speak in a gentle manner. This helps you change your attitude and tone of voice and may divert bad feelings.

Or, knowing your mate wants some quiet time after arriving home from work, you won't be surprised if he or she goes off to a room to be alone for a while.

As you each become aware of what will make the other happier in the marriage, you'll know what to do and not do. Instead of just stabbing in the dark, hoping to do the right things, you'll have a better idea of what actions and attitudes are needed.

By the way, go through this process about once a month for the first several months or until this is a natural part of your life with each other.

Use First-Quality Materials

A few years ago we surveyed 186 couples to find out what they thought were the most important ingredients for a lasting marriage. We sent an extensive questionnaire to couples in mid-life or beyond who had been married at least fifteen years. When we compiled the results, the following ten characteristics headed the list:[4]

1. Commitment to marriage (not only committed to stay married, but committed to enrich the marriage).

2. Good communication (able to dialog with each other).

3. Vital spiritual life (at least one and sometimes both partners were spiritually alive).

4. Effective conflict resolution (able to mutually work out differences).

5. Positive impact from other people (maintaining constructive friendships).

6. Sexual intimacy (mutually satisfying sexual relationship).

7. Fun, leisure, and humor (time was allocated for recreation and a sense of humor).

8. Realistic expectations (accepting and enjoying each other).

9. Serving each other (doing things to please each other on a basis of mutuality).

10. Personal growth (growing as an individual to bring a freshness to the marriage).

These traits would be good building materials as you reconstruct your marriage. A quality building is not made from shoddy materials and workmanship; neither is a good marriage.

In that sense, marriage is also like baking. For example, to make a torte you need the best ingredients. You can't say, "I don't have enough flour so I'll just use cornstarch and I don't have any fresh fruit so I'll use some canned fruit cocktail." You have to use what the recipe calls for. You also have to use the right procedures. You can't just gather all the ingredients and mix them together at one time. Unless you have the correct ingredients, in the correct amounts, and put them together in the correct steps, you won't have a torte. You may have something edible—if you're starving—but it won't be a delicate pastry.

In one sense, gourmet cooking is a better metaphor than construction work for marriage. Building a house is a one-time effort. If you make a mistake, you live with the consequences. But in baking you can learn from each experience. If your first torte doesn't turn out exactly right you can figure out what you did wrong and improve on it the next time you try.

The same is true of all the ingredients in marriage. If your first attempt at meeting your spouse's needs is a disaster, you can figure out what went wrong and improve on it the next time. The ingredients that go into a marriage won't be perfect all the time. You can aim for perfection, but in this lifetime you and your mate will never reach it. So give yourselves credit for the progress you are making in choosing the best ingredients and adding them in the right order and keep working *toward* perfection.

Correct Problems Right Away

You already know what happens when you let problems slide. They don't go away. They get worse and cause complications. In rebuilding your marriage, work on problems as soon as they arise. Don't simply patch something without correcting the basic problem. Everybody knows that it makes no sense to repair the ceiling plaster without first repairing the leak in the roof that caused the damage.

At one of the churches we pastored, the men of the congregation were constructing the new sanctuary themselves. A few retired men worked nearly every day, other men worked on their days off, and many others came in the evenings. George, an elderly man who had been a housebuilder in earlier days, came as often as his strength allowed.

George was proud of his work and didn't realize that he no longer was able to do a precise job. The other builders were very particular about their work and wanted each detail on their church done as perfectly as possible. The man who was the unofficial foreman always tried to give George jobs where accuracy wasn't a factor.

One day, however, the foreman was not present and George was. George spent several hours rough-framing two doorways. After he left, the foreman arrived and couldn't believe his eyes! Both doorways were so crooked that minor adjustments could not correct the problem. A decision had to be made. Should they leave the work as it was and try to compensate for the errors, or should they risk hurting George's feelings and redo both doorways? They decided to redo all the work. Far into the night, men took apart and redid what George had done.

Fortunately, George wasn't able to come back for several days. By the time he did, the building had progressed far enough that he never knew his rough framing had been redone. If it had been left as it was, the two doors at the front of the sanctuary would be out of line to this day.

Add Decorator Touches

You can build a plain concrete block house with a door and some windows, or you can add some enhancement. The plain house will shelter you, but the house with some added features will bring more enjoyment.

After you get your marriage on solid footing, think of ways you can enrich your relationship. Add a few touches of interest. Plan little pleasures and surprises for your mate. They may be as simple as an unexpected note or an inexpensive treat.

Put romance back into your relationship. Go carefully, however. Your mate may not be able to rush into playful intimacy with you right away. Intimacy needs to grow slowly, as when you first met.

First use eye contact. Then begin gentle touches. When both of you are ready, hugging, kissing, and caressing may be added. Finally, you both may want sexual intercourse. Don't be discouraged if it takes some weeks to get to the last stage. Love can be shown in many other ways.

For a long time our culture has believed that women wanted romance and affection while men only wanted sexual intercourse. Many of today's males want to be let out of that stereotype. They have learned to be more sensitive and aware of feelings.

Also, a psychological change takes place in men during their mid-years, and they actually become more feeling oriented than in their younger years.[5] They like to be caressed and hugged and given a light kiss. Touching doesn't necessarily have to lead to intercourse for them to feel loved and cared for.

Both men and women enjoy intercourse as well as romantic tenderness. But both also take pleasure in simply being close.

Don't be disheartened if you or your mate don't have intense love feelings for each other when you first come back together. You've been battered and bruised, and you may need some healing time before feelings return.

As you learn that you can trust each other, your emotions will become more loving. If you carry out loving actions—even when you don't feel loving—feelings will eventually come along.

As your marriage becomes more steady, look for new ways to grow. Take on small challenges and keep adding to your rebuilt structure. You may decide to build more than a plain little marriage— perhaps you can have a magnificent mansion!

Chapter 19

Encourage Hurts to Heal

• • •

DIANE KEPT PUTTING her hand to her heart as she went about dusting her house. She felt as if someone was twisting a knife inside the pulsing muscles of her heart.

The pain started when she found out that her husband had been involved in an affair. It was over now, Charlie said, and he seemed truly sorry it had ever happened. But it wasn't over for Diane.

Every time she looked at Charlie, ugly thoughts raced into her mind and sent stabbing pain straight to her heart again. *How could he desecrate their relationship?* she wondered. *And why? She had been a good wife. What excuse could he possibly have?*

She became bitter even though she didn't want to. She looked at him through narrowed eyes with her mouth set in a firm, straight line. When he tried to touch her, she pulled away. She turned her back to him in bed. Sometimes she wondered if she even loved him any more, and then she'd realize that she truly did. But he had hurt her so much!

She started thinking wicked, revengeful thoughts about the

other woman and even wished she could put a curse on her. This wasn't the Diane she knew; she didn't like the hatred growing inside her, but she didn't know how to stop it.

The pain! It was becoming unbearable. She had to get some relief. She looked for verses in the Bible that would give her comfort, but her heartache took up so much room that she had no place to put anything else.

Finally the agony overwhelmed her. She had to have help. She found a counselor who helped her acknowledge her wounds and showed her what to do to help them heal. As she learned more about herself, she also understood Charlie better. She realized that he did love her and actually needed her to show more love to him.

Diane finally came to the place where she could start to forgive Charlie for the affair. Each time an ugly memory came to her mind, she would deliberately say, "I love him and I forgive him." Gradually her heart pain disappeared. It took a long time to be completely cured, but each day she made steady progress.

Honesty Pays

Even if you and your mate are together again, your lives probably are not completely whole and healthy. You have bruises and wounds that need to heal.

A first step toward healing is to admit you have been hurt and to identify the injuries. Some mates will be willing to talk a great deal; others will find it too painful and too out of character to discuss the offenses in detail.

When you talk about your hurts, don't attack your mate. Calmly state how you've been injured. As you speak, talk about *your* feelings and observations instead of assaulting your mate with "you did this or that" and "you are this or that."

Say "I feel . . ." in place of "You make me feel. . . ." Or say "I feel insecure when. . . ," not "You caused. . . ."

When you level with your mate, don't level him or her. Your

mate is not a hideous monster that needs to be flattened. Your honesty sessions will be much more rewarding if done in kindness and love.

Honesty is a two-way street. If you state your grievances, allow your mate the same opportunity. Be ready to admit your part in the failure of your relationship. It may be hard for you to hear, but listen to what your mate thinks went wrong.

Forgiveness Is Freeing

In *Forgive & Forget: Healing the Hurts We Don't Deserve*, Lewis Smedes reminds us that forgiving is usually done slowly and a little at a time.[1] Often forgiving is also done in confusion:

> Forgiving is wisdom's high art; most of us who work at it, however, are muddlers and bunglers. We usually move toward forgiving in the cross-currents of our confusion.[2]

As you get to the place where you want to forgive your mate, don't be hard on yourself if it doesn't happen easily. Just remember that forgiveness *is* eventually possible as you honestly work through the violations against you.

Perhaps it will help you to forgive if you realize you can do it because Christ has forgiven *your* wrongs. A key verse about forgiveness is "Be kind and loving to each other. Forgive each other just as God forgave you in Christ" (Eph. 4:32 NCV).

In *Healing for Damaged Emotions* Dr. David Seamands tells us to "get out of the setting right and getting even business, and into the forgiving and the loving business."[3]

Forgiving does not mean that you somehow erase history. What has happened is a fact. But as you heal, you will eventually reach the place where memories no longer feel like knives in your heart.

When you forgive, you must also give up your resentments. If you nurse the wrongs your mate did to you, they only grow larger and stronger. If you keep bringing up the affair or other events that disrupted your marriage you are conveying to your mate that you have not genuinely forgiven.

Getting rid of malice will give you a light heart. Carrying a grudge will only keep you earthbound when instead you could be flying free as an eagle.

Memories Can Be Healed

The problem with memories is that they aren't just vague thoughts. They trigger your emotions so it feels as if the event is happening again at that very moment. Each time you relive an unhappy experience, you are wounded anew.

How do you get your memories to quit gnawing at your heart and mind?

Those gruesome memories will eventually fade if you and your mate are sincerely working on the healing process. In *The Myth of the Greener Grass* J. Allan Petersen says, "Certainly where trust has been broken there may be questions for a period of time, occasional twinges of doubt, or echoes, but these will pass if there is a mutual effort to improve the marital relationship."[4]

God can make the pain of your bad memories subside. As you pray about your hurts, imagine that God is beside you and that together you are looking at the hurtful event as if it were just now happening. Visualize yourself asking for his help. Then pray for him to touch your mind and soul in the days to come.

Time is on your side in the healing of memories. If you deliberately confront your hurts, forgive them, and ask for God's healing, the memories will come less often and the hurt will lessen.

Imagine that your mind is a tape player. When an old hurt or a new suspicion starts to play its ugly song, just insert a different "tape"—the tape that assures you of God's love and your improving marital situation. If your mate is giving you positive signals about the progress of your relationship, concentrate on these signs rather than on the old painful memories.

Change Old Patterns of Living

Rick and Stacy sat side-by-side in a coffee shop booth enjoying a quick lunch together. Their arms were touching as they studied the menus. After placing their orders they chatted about how their morning had gone. The waitress interrupted occasionally to serve them, but their attention was on each other.

As they finished lunch, Stacy said, "I'm so glad we're taking time out of the day to see each other. It seems so long to go without seeing you from morning until night."

"I like it too. It makes me feel much closer to you," Rick added.

Outside the coffee shop, they each went to their cars to return to their respective jobs. "See ya tonight at home," Rick said as he kissed Stacy on the cheek.

Rick and Stacy's relationship hasn't always been so cozy. Two years ago they were both concentrating so much on their jobs, household responsibilities, and social obligations that they didn't make much time for each other.

Stacy began to feel that Rick thought of her only as someone to do the household tasks, provide sex, and help him look good socially. She was getting no nourishment from their marriage, and her emptiness became her weak spot.

When one of Stacy's coworkers took an interest in her, Stacy fell into an insidious trap. Steve made her feel pretty and important. They started going to lunch together just to talk. Then they began to take short rides after work.

One late afternoon they stopped at a secluded spot in a large park. Steve made bold sexual advances toward Stacy, and she got scared. She insisted that he stop immediately and take her to her car.

Stacy drove home as the sun set in front of her. Brilliant orange streaks beamed into the clouds on all sides around her. The brightness outside was a stark contrast to the dismal darkness inside her soul. She realized that her relationship with Steve was absolutely wrong and that she was in almost over her head. She knew she had to get out now.

She was starting dinner when Rick arrived home. She got the meal in the oven and then, with a trembling voice, said, "Rick, we need to talk." He sat with her in the family room as she tearfully told him what had been going on with Steve.

Rick was shaken and hurt. He walked around in circles and ran his fingers through his hair. Then he went for a walk by himself.

He did a lot of mental wrestling as he walked. Eventually he began to see that their situation wasn't hopeless. Stacy had come home instead of leaving him. She'd told him about the entanglement with Steve instead of hiding it any longer. She had been involved with Steve emotionally, but not sexually. She was extremely sorry and wanted to strengthen their marriage.

When he returned to the house he assured Stacy that he forgave her and wanted to do his part to get their marriage back on sure footing again. They decided they needed to do more things together and to do specific things every day to let the other know that he or she was loved.

They each had jobs that allowed them to take long lunch hours, so they agreed that at least twice a week they would meet for lunch. Sometimes they brought sack lunches and ate in a park.

They decided to help each other with the house and yard work on the weekends so they could be together. By working together they got the jobs done more quickly and found free time to go on inexpensive "adventures" nearly every week.

Rick and Stacy had to practice their new lifestyle for several weeks before it became a habit, but now they can't bear the thought of living the old way. "And to think we almost lost each other because of bad patterns we had set up," they say solemnly.

Create Healing Habits

Heal your old hurts by breaking harmful habits and creating healthy ones. Substitute activities that strengthen your marriage for ones that cause it to deteriorate. Practice new, kind ways of speaking to each other. Show a little love every day. Have some fun experiences—they don't have to be costly to provide enjoyment.

As you produce a new design for your relationship you will not only enrich your marriage, you will also replace ugly memories with new, happier ones.

When an old hurt starts throbbing again, go back to the Great Physician and let him apply his healing ointment. Remind yourself that these old memories have been cared for and that you don't have to let them hurt you.

Chapter 20

Invest for a Lifetime

• • •

MARRIAGE RESTORATION ISN'T a once-for-all-time project. You can never say you're finished. No marriage is ever
complete, not even one that has never been threatened as yours has.
There is always more work and more growing to be done.

Wayne learned this the hard way. Although his wife, Jenny, was
a professing Christian, she always seemed to be meeting new men and
falling in love. Often the infatuation turned into a sexual relationship.
When Wayne accused Jenny of being nothing but a common slut, she
shook her finger at him and said, "I have nothing to keep myself pure
for. You're no husband to me. You're gone most of the time, and when
you are home, you're in your workshop. You don't go to bed when I
do, and you're always gone before I wake up."

Pastor Bob helped them reach an uneasy truce when they went
to him for help. They agreed to keep living together after Jenny
promised not to get involved with any other men and Wayne promised
to pay more attention to her.

Wayne was relieved when Jenny once again seemed to be trying
to be a homemaker and his wife. She kept her attentions off other men
and concentrated on being attractive to Wayne. It wasn't long,
though, before Wayne began to slip on his part of the bargain. His

company assigned him to a special project that required long hours and when he got home, he didn't want to go straight to sleep—he wanted to putter in his workshop.

Jenny frequently went to the site where Wayne was working to maintain a connection with him. She'd take him a cold drink and just chat for a few minutes. Wayne barely acknowledged her presence. He quickly gulped down whatever she brought and then plunged back into his work.

Some of the other men, though, took time to notice Jenny. They kidded her about bringing them something to drink too. So she started making iced tea in a large thermos and giving some to all the men. They would take a few minutes to talk with her while Wayne kept at his work. One particular man, Rusty, spent lots of time talking to Jenny, and she thoroughly enjoyed his attention.

Late one night Wayne tromped into the house and found a note propped against a pop bottle on the table:

> Rusty and I have left town. He won't be at work any-
> more. He really loves me, and we want to be together.
> Don't bother trying to bring me back this time.
> Your formerly lonely wife,
> Jenny.

Even though it was after midnight, Wayne frantically called Pastor Bob. He told him his story and they agreed to meet in the morning. As they talked the next day, Wayne began to see that he had been extremely careless in taking care of his marriage. Unfortunately, Jenny never did come back to Wayne, and they are divorced.

Increase Your Assets

Coming together again is not all there is to a successful relationship. You must not forget that you're in a rebuilding process that requires alertness and enthusiasm every day. You'll need a lifetime commitment.

Don't let that overwhelm you. You only have to live one day at a time, and you don't have to meet these demands in your own strength. God will empower you for the job. He will help you "take a new grip with your tired hands [and] stand firm on your shaky legs" (Hebrews 12:12 TLB).

Perhaps you are starting out with only one asset—your willingness to try. But from a feeble start you can, with God's help, build something strong and beautiful.

Storing Up Treasures

Rebuilding your marriage is similar to investing in a savings account or money market fund. You don't have to make one large deposit all at once; you can add to it as you go.

In rebuilding a sound marriage, you can make deposits into your account many times a day. Each time you do something favorable to or for your mate, you are adding to your investment.

The difference between investing in a bank account and investing in your marriage is that your marriage is a living organism. You and your spouse can interact with each other as you respond, react, and cooperate. Money has no feeling; your mate does. Money is temporary; your mate is eternal.

What Can You Deposit?

What each couple invests in their marriage-rebuilding account will vary according to the unique character of the two people in the relationship. There are, however, some investments everyone can make:

Improved Attitudes

Are you an optimistic person? Is your glass half empty or half full? Are you interested in others or consumed with your own concerns? Are you suspicious of others' motives and actions or do you grant the benefit of a doubt? Can you tolerate a difference in opinions or preferences? Do you value another's privacy? Are you cheerful and encouraging or crabby and complaining? Do you affirm or criticize others (your mate, in particular)? Do you boss and nag until people want to shake free from your dominance?

As you can see, a great number of attitudes affect our lives and relationships. Since you want to restore your marriage, you'll want to develop good attitudes in everything you do. Your mate will be watching you. He or she will be much more desirous to work on the marriage with you if you're a pleasant, upbeat person.

You won't regret investing in healthy attitudes. As your investment grows, your mate will enjoy you more, other people will enjoy you more, and you'll even like yourself better. You really do get a good return on your investment when you develop positive attitudes.

Beneficial Words

Some of us talk too much; others don't say enough. What some of us say is worthwhile; what others say is nearly useless or very damaging. The right use of words can help a marriage grow strong; the wrong use of words can destroy it.

James in the New Testament reminds us:

> We all stumble in many ways. If anyone does not stumble in what he says, he is a perfect man, able to bridle the whole body as well.
>
> Now if we put the bits into the horses' mouths so that they may obey us, we direct their entire body as well.
>
> Behold, the ships also, though they are so great and are driven by strong winds, are still directed by a very small rudder. . . .
>
> So also the tongue is a small part of the body, and yet it [is capable] of great things (James 3:2–5 NASB).

Words reveal attitudes, so use words to bless and encourage. Even if you are directing an employee or instructing your child, and especially when you're speaking to your mate, kind words get positive results.

Remember to *use* words. If you are the strong, silent type you may forget that your mate isn't a mind reader. Talk to your mate so that she or he isn't left watching a silent movie with no subtitles. Communication is one way to feel close to each other.

For those of you for whom talking is easy, don't forget to shut off the flow once in awhile. Give your husband or wife a chance to use words too.

Acts of Kindness

You are known by what you do. Good intentions only go a little way. If you don't carry them out, you are soon known as a pretender or a procrastinator.

Your behavior for investing in your marriage covers everything from common courtesies in daily life to specific, creative deeds to show your love.

I have recently undergone breast cancer surgery and intensive chemotherapy, which debilitated me for over a year. I could hardly care for myself, let alone keep up household duties or go about my counseling and writing ministry.

Jim let me know immediately that his major priority was my recovery. He waited on me when I couldn't care for myself. He took on the cooking, cleaning, laundry, grocery shopping, and managing the household. He did my share of the office and speaking ministry. He went with me for innumerable doctors' visits and tests.

He was my cheerleader, encouraging me that together we would make it through this ordeal. He said he didn't mind my lopsided chest or my balding head. He helped me go for short walks outdoors by letting me hang on to him. He listened to my moaning and groaning when I was too sick to be a nice person.

One of the most outstanding things Jim did for me was to dress a large, ugly wound where my breast had been. He did this for over nine months! I had complications, and a gaping hole developed in my chest following surgery. Every day Jim tenderly cleaned and wrapped that repulsive opening.

When I would thank him for all he was doing for me, he would say, "I'm glad to do it. I'm here to serve you."

What if, at the beginning of the cancer experience, he had said he would help me and then had ignored me most of the time?

His kind words would have been like a helium-filled balloon that escapes a child's grasp and floats upward out of reach toward endless space. Jim's loving actions conveyed more meaning than any words could have.

What can you do every day that shows your love for your mate and makes your marriage enjoyable? You're a busy person, but if you want a restored marriage you can't afford to neglect doing things for and with your spouse.

Deposits Now Pay Dividends Later

Remember the parable of the master who was going on a journey and distributed money among his servants? One man hid his money and did nothing with it until the master returned. The other two men invested their money and had a multiplied amount to give to their master when he came back.

The two servants who increased their money were praised. The servant who buried his money had it taken from him and was thrown out of his master's presence.[1]

Your opportunity to rebuild your marriage is like the money given to the servants. Don't bury your opportunity; use it. Make investments every day that will pay dividends of a stronger marriage. If you put more in, you'll get more out.

What you get from your investment in your marriage, however, is more than mere dollars and cents. A happy marriage benefits you, your mate, your children, your extended family, and everyone else in your world. Their lives will be healthier because yours is. An enjoyable feature of a savings account or money market fund is that you begin to get interest on your money as soon as it's deposited. The same is true when you invest in your marriage restoration project.

Not only will you enjoy the benefits now, but you'll also have profits later. "Increase" is a key word of investment. It's like a reward for faithfully storing up good things. Increase and dividends are what you'll get from rebuilding your marriage.

Since our marriage in 1954, each anniversary impresses us with the rewards of having lived so many years together. We used to grimace at Robert Browning's sentiment, "Grow old along with me, the best is yet to be." We wondered, *What's so great about growing old together?*

Our real question was *What's so great about growing old?* Since we can't escape growing older, we're finding it's a great adventure to do it together.

There's something comforting about coming home to someone who has known you since you were a well-intentioned, but immature pup. You have a long history together. You know what the other's parents were like. You shared joy when your kids were born and sorrow when those kids broke your heart.

You saw your mate make mistakes and learn from them. You know what it has taken for your spouse to get this far in life. You knew each other when you had more hair and a bouncier spring in your step. Just a phrase or a certain look triggers a whole panorama of connections between the two of you. You have your little private jokes.

Life may be hard, but you have someone who has been over the same bumps and is willing to keep on going with you.

We sincerely hope that you and your mate have the opportunity to enjoy an ongoing marriage. We want you to discover that "the best is yet to be."

May God bless and empower you.

Part 5

TO PASTORS
AND
COUNSELORS

Chapter 21

Work for Restoration, Not Divorce

◆ ◆ ◆

A FEW YEARS AGO I was getting ready to speak in one of the largest Baptist churches in Southern California. The man who was to introduce me was a divorce lawyer. He leaned over to me and said, "What you're going to be talking about this morning is very important for our people. Looking around the congregation, I see more than fifty of my clients who are in the process of divorce."

Since the Second World War, Americans have watched the divorce rate rise until its peak in the early eighties at slightly over 50 percent. In other words, if a hundred people in an average town got married in a given year, fifty people in the same town would get divorced.

In the early fifties Christians were quite smug about the spiraling divorce rate, thinking it happened only to "those people" on the outside. Some Christian writers even said that truly committed Christians would never get a divorce. They believed the slogan, "The family that prays together stays together." However, by the late seventies the divorce rate for Christians began catching up to that of the general population.

In the sixties and early seventies, pastors I surveyed thought that the divorce problem was outside of the church. Their simple response was, "I don't have anything to do with people who are divorced or remarried."

The fantasy of a Christian subculture without divorce or remarriage is no longer possible. Divorce has penetrated even the smallest towns and remotest parts of our country so that no pastor can put his head in the sand and say, "I don't have to be involved in this problem."

Marital stress even among churchgoers is not a figment of imagination. It's real life. It's tough life. It affects everything that happens in the individual family as well as in the church, community, extended family, and in generation after generation as people carry with them the baggage from a difficult family life.

So the question is, how do we deal with this reality? How can we counsel, put programs into action, and work together as a team of caring specialists to heal sick marriages and steer those at the point of divorce onto a course toward marital harmony?

The rest of this chapter suggests a perspective for counselors, pastors, small group leaders, elders, deacons—in short, anyone who is trying to rebuild marriages, reduce the divorce rate, or soothe the giant pain divorce is causing all across our country.

Counsel Toward Restoration, Not Divorce

Most couples in failing marriages will try several do-it-yourself approaches to help their marriage before they seek professional counseling. By the time they reach out for help, the situation has usually deteriorated so much that they probably are talking about divorce and one of them may have moved into separate quarters.

Many of these marriages appear to have little or no potential for reconciliation or stabilization. Because of a couple's longstanding problems, their disillusionment with attempted solutions, and their sheer fatigue, counselors frequently are tempted to concur with the bleak assessment of the marriage and encourage the couple to get divorced, accept God's forgiveness, and press on with life.

One of the most difficult battles we face in our office at Mid-Life Dimensions is that of encouraging people to keep working toward reconciliation and stabilization while Christian counselors and pastors are encouraging these people to divorce.

Many of these marriages could be saved if counselors or pastors understood developmental issues and were willing to consider additional approaches to counseling, which we'll be looking at in the rest of this chapter.

Our office is currently achieving about a 50 percent reconciliation rate for marriages that have been written off by most people. We consider a marriage reconciled when the couple report they are together again and are both resolving problems in their marriage.

When counseling a troubled couple, keep in mind the following ideas:

Divorce Is Not the Best Answer

Although the Bible permits divorce under certain conditions, it never suggests it as the best solution. People who divorce frequently believe they have solved the problem. They are, however, likely to marry another person very similar to the former mate and relate to that person in many of the same destructive ways as in the previous marriage. In addition, he or she may carry a haunting sense of guilt and hear the probing question, "Could I have made my first marriage work if only I had done something differently?"

It is important for the counselor to ask, "Am I pushing these people toward divorce because I am frustrated at the length of the healing process or the depth of the problems?"

Everyone's Not Getting a Divorce

Marital fidelity is being barraged by the idea that "everyone's doing it"—everyone is playing around and everyone is breaking up. Even many Christians feel justified in leaving their marriage or having an affair if their mate doesn't make them happy. One man told us, "My wife hasn't met my basic needs for the last five years. So, of course, I got involved with another woman. After all, what does my wife expect? . . . It's really her fault I had the affair, you know."

Some cynics are claiming, as they look at the high divorce rate, that expecting one marriage to last a life-time is a bankrupt idea. It's interesting to note, however, that marriage is more popular than ever. Even though the divorce rate is hovering around the 50 percent mark, a greater percentage of our population is married today than ever before.[1]

From our study of couples whose marriages have survived, and from the many couples we counsel, we have learned that successful couples are willing to say, "We don't care what everyone else is doing, we're going to make this marriage work."[2] These couples made this pronouncement in spite of the fact that divorce for married persons forty to sixty years of age rose more than 50 percent between 1968 and 1978.[3]

To survive, every marriage must develop the strength to swim against the tide.

An Affair or Separation Can Be an Opportunity for Growth and Reconciliation

Affairs often start because of a vacuum in one's personality or in the marital relationship. If the vacuum can be filled in legitimate ways, the need and urgency for the affair disappears. Counseling is more productive when it deals with the causes of the vacuum than when it commiserates about the evil of the affair.

A separation can provide the distance that facilitates healing, but a separation does not require that one of the partners move out of the city, state, or even out of the house. Even "slight" separations can be extremely helpful if a couple is at the point of desperation.

A separate bedroom within the house can be identified as a retreat for one of the mates. And short-term separations can be accomplished through fishing trips, church retreats, and visits with old friends (of the same sex, of course).

The counselor should help slow down the process toward divorce. If separation must take place, encourage small, incremental steps. The fewer bridges burned, the easier it is to be reconciled.

Help the Counselee to Focus on the Mate

Counseling should work not only on the counselee's general well-being, but also on enabling the person to meet the needs of his or her mate. We believe that marriages are primarily held together because people meet each other's needs. Therefore, helping the counselee to understand the mate's needs and to actively meet those needs will provide a later basis for reconciliation.

Counsel from a Developmental Perspective

The study of adult development is a rather new phenomenon. Before the late 1920s, it was generally assumed that adults could not learn or change after their early twenties. In 1928,[4] Edward Thorndike shocked the educational world with his studies of adults in their thirties. He discovered that they *were* capable of continued learning.

Charlotte Buhler[5] was one of the early researchers studying the process of adult development (1939). Erik Erikson (1950),[6] Robert Havighurst (1953),[7] Bernice Neugarten (1964),[8] and a host of others in the late sixties through the nineties, have expanded the research and study of adult development and learning from an educational, spiritual/moral, and psychological point of view.

As a result, researchers have divided the adult era into many sub-periods. Adulthood, which had been considered a very stable period, is now seen as a time of growth with several important times of change.

A large group of researchers and writers, such as Alan B. Knox,[9]

Daniel J. Levinson,[10] Roger Gould,[11] Marjorie Lowenthal,[12] and many others, have helped to delineate these adult stages more precisely. It is now commonly accepted that the adult lifespan consists of a young adult era, a mid-life era, and an aging era. Each of these broad stages is then divided even more finely.

All through the adult stages of life a process of reassessment takes place as people realize they are moving into a new era. At each stage they ask, "Who am I?" "What should I do with my life?" and "How should I relate to others and to God?" These questions are asked by teens becoming young adults, young adults coming to mid-life, and mid-life adults turning older.

In addition to the normal developmental process of moving from one era to another, people also experience physical aging, work pressures, increased community and social responsibilities, an awareness of the shortness of life, and a decreasing amount of personal intimacy, particularly within marriage.

All of these developmental changes, cultural pressures, and internal questions may cause problems in marriage. Each partner may be so consumed with his or her own developmental concerns that no energy is left to maintain the marriage.

Counsel with an Insight into Changing Needs

In addition to the internal factors that may cause marriages to erode, there are also external forces at work.

For centuries marriage was necessary for physical survival; then it became a primary unit of economic survival. Some sociologists believe that in primitive cultures the word *love* may not have been associated with marriage because couples united for other reasons.[13]

In our culture people don't usually marry for economic or political advantages or to have children to work the land. Most people marry for love, companionship, and a secure relationship in a lonely and uncertain world.

Today's marriage partners have to be concerned not only about physical survival, financial stability, and family harmony, they also have to be good listeners, sensitive, caring, understanding, and terrific sexual partners with great-looking bodies! A contemporary marriage partner has to meet many of a mate's needs for friendship that in past days were met by the extended family or by church and community friends.

This century has seen a dramatic lengthening of American life expectancy. As recently as 1900, the average length of life was only about forty-nine years. In the eighties, however, average life expectancy rose to over seventy years.[14]

In past generations, unhappily married fifty-year-olds figured they didn't have many more years to put up with each other. Today's dissatisfied fifty-year-olds know they may have twenty to forty more years of potential marital misery.

Counsel with an Individual's History in Mind

All of us bring problems into marriage because we bring ourselves. We are a combination of strengths and weaknesses, positive experiences and crushing blows. We are people who have a light, transparent side as well as a dark, secretive side. We carry our total selves into the marriage relationship. Any unresolved problem, inadequacy, or family dysfunction from our past may be the seed of marital breakup.

I discovered in my fifties that I never fully trusted that Sally would not abandon me once she found out how inadequate I really was. My parents were emotionally divorced from the very first day of their marriage, and I thought that emotional distancing in a marriage was normal. As a result, I never fully committed myself to Sally. I felt deep down inside that sooner or later she would leave me, so I didn't invest everything in our marriage because that way I wouldn't get hurt too much when she abandoned me.[15]

Sometimes marriage dissatisfaction can be traced directly to dysfunctional baggage carried from childhood or teen years.

Frequently we hear a story like that of Ken, an insecure man married to a strong woman. In the early years Ken was glad that Carol helped him with many of his decisions, but in his late thirties he began to throw off all mentors. He resented having his wife continually "mothering" him.

In counseling it became apparent that their problems went back to their development in homes with dominant mothers. Ken had not realized that he married Carol partly because he admired her leadership abilities. She had learned from her mother to take control. He had learned from his father to be passive. It seemed like a perfect match.

As Ken grew older, however, he wanted to take more responsibility for personal decisions. Ken and Carol had to work on a new style of leadership to keep their marriage from disintegrating.[16]

Counsel with an Awareness of Predictable Divorce Ages

Courtship and the early married years include the new and novel—getting to know each other, exploring sex together, launching a new career, bringing children into the world, and rearing them. Then the focus moves to buying a home and getting the "extras"—a second car, a boat, a video cassette recorder, special trips—those things that mean "we have arrived."

Tragically, a subtle shift takes place that may go unnoticed until the middle years. The couple increasingly focuses on everyday activities and the accumulation of things rather than on each other. Couples justify this outward focus because "we're buying a house," "raising children," "starting a business," "buying the luxuries of life."

Suddenly a chilling realization descends. Though once deeply in love with each other, the couple has become boring people with no common interests except their children, investments, and properties. They have fallen into routines that are necessary but hum-drum and lifeless.

Another blow to marriage may be the awareness that it is turning out just like that of their parents'. They had promised each other that theirs would be different. Instead, they realize they married someone just like their father-in-law or mother-in-law, which isn't what either of them had in mind!

The apparent dissatisfaction with marriage is not a new phenomenon. A Detroit study done in the early 1960s showed that only 6 percent of the wives were satisfied with their marriages after twenty-two years.[17]

Also in the sixties, psychologist and columnist Dr. Joyce Brothers stated, "Marriage is a 'quiet hell' for about half of American couples, . . . four of twelve marriages will end in divorce, while another six become loveless 'utilitarian' relationships to protect children, property, shared concerns, and other goals."[18]

In a study of 2,000 married couples, Richard Strauss reported in 1973 that 60 percent of men would not marry the same partner if they had it to do over.[19] Some research is indeed pessimistic about the future of our western society in general and marriage specifically, but in spite of these gloomy views, there has been a definite turn from the seventies "me-ism" to concern for the group and marriage and family. That's good news!

The First Year

The most dangerous year for a potential divorce is the first. There are many reasons for the high first-year failure rate, but most boil down to inadequate preparation. Couples are carefully rehearsed on where to stand for the marriage ceremony, but few get the counseling necessary to help them deal with their own personal family history and prepare them for the realities of their own marriage.

During my many years as a pastor, I said to the congregation, to singles' groups, and to junior-high and high-school students that it was important to get premarital counseling. Ideally, I wanted to see the couple in the early stages of a relationship—while it was simply a serious friendship. Coming to see me didn't mean they were announcing a date to get married. But early visits gave me an opportunity to help each of them accelerate their emotional maturity so that, whomever they married, they would be better prepared.

In each church I pastored, I encouraged those in leadership to pass a resolution that no one on the pastoral staff could perform marriages for couples who would not commit themselves to six to eight hours of premarital counseling over a three-month period. Plus, the couples had to read several books, take appropriate tests, and follow through on any recommended referrals.

The result was that a number of couples did not get married right away—some never did. Some spent more time growing; others discovered they were not right for each other.

It is time for counselors, pastors, parents, wedding coordinators, and church officials to band together to insist on serious, in-depth premarital counseling so that we can head off the tragically high divorce rate of the first year.

The Late Twenties and Early Thirties

By this age many couples have been married about seven years. It isn't that seven years of marriage is automatically a bad time, but a divorce is more likely during a developmental reassessment time, one of which occurs at the end of the twenties or in the early thirties.

During the late teens and early twenties, individuals usually choose what they want to do with their lives. During that time people often decide to get married and start their family and career. All looks well until they get to the late twenties and begin to ask themselves, "Am I really on target? Am I accomplishing the goals I thought I would accomplish? Is my marriage really as satisfying and fulfilling as I hoped?"

If the answer to any of these questions is no, the partner may look at his or her mate and think that someone new would improve the situation.

Couples struggling with the question of whether or not to stay together usually do so alone. The rest of the community sees them as "well established" and out of danger. Everything seems to be O.K. Unfortunately, this can be a very dangerous period for marriages and is a crucial time for the community, church, counselors, and other leaders to plan marriage enrichment seminars or special classes to help couples work through this questioning period.

The Mid-Life Era

The time of highest risk for married couples is at mid-life. The potential for depression, anger, frustration, and rebellion is great. If one or both of the partners are experiencing mid-life crisis, their lives will be affected not only physically, but also socially, culturally, spiritually, and occupationally. Mid-life is a time when people reach the peak of the mountain and look back to see where they have come from and look forward to what lies ahead. How people evaluate accomplishments, hopes, and dreams will determine whether life ahead will be an exhilarating challenge or simply a demoralizing expanse that must be drearily traversed.

Mid-life, which is roughly ages thirty-five to fifty-five, was previously thought to be a settled time but now is seen as a potentially tumultuous era for marriage. It is during this period that people reassess their personal values and goals related to marriage, career, friendships, and social commitments, as well as God.

Mid-life has several sub-stages. The mid-thirties male, who quite often is an aggressive, single-focused individual trying to make his mark in the world, is very different from the early forties male who is wondering what life is all about and which values and lifestyles he should change. The man in his fifties is different from both groups. He has mellowed and is more willing to invest himself in the lives of younger people.

Mid-life men quite often experience a shock of realism about their careers. For the first time they may come to understand they're not going to go as far as they had dreamed. Frequently mid-life husbands who are angry about their career or other facets of life will project that anger onto their marriage. They may blame their wife for the limitations and frustrations they are experiencing.

A mid-life wife may feel that her husband is keeping her in a mother-only role. If their children are in high school or moving out of the nest, her mothering job is coming to an end. This loss may affect her self-identity and self-worth and may breed resentment toward her husband if he wants her to function only as a mother.

She may be tired of putting up with an absentee husband consumed by his career goals, and her own sense of cultural displacement may be setting in as she realizes that society no longer considers her "young and beautiful." The feeling of loss she experiences in many areas causes her to reassess her values.

Many couples of various ages feel trapped into pretending they like each other, themselves, and what they do. They live out a farce, acting as if all is well in their marriage and in their individual lives.

Changing Life Questions

Since the adult years have several reassessment times, the marital relationship will likely need to be readjusted to fit the changes at each transition.

The questions asked in the early twenties are future-oriented: "Who am I? What shall I do with my life? With whom shall I relate?" Most people marry during this early twenties adjustment period.

The questions asked in the late twenties and early thirties are progression-oriented: "How am I doing with the choices I have made? Am I progressing fast enough? What are the areas that need to be corrected in order to accomplish my life goals?"

At mid-life, the questions are now-oriented: "Who am I now? Who am I becoming? What will my values be? Am I satisfied with my career? Who will my friends be? Am I contented in my marriage? How does God fit into my life? How is my life making a difference in the world?"[20]

The perspective is, "Life is running out too fast. I need to make corrections *NOW!* I only have twenty to thirty more good years left."

At each developmental reassessment stage, marriage will take on a slightly different form because of the personal growth of each mate.

Counsel with Long-Term Patience

Keep the Counselee Focused

One of the major problems in the long-term counseling of an unstable marriage is that frequently the people lose perspective and give up hope. Each new event produces trauma—something bad happens at work, a letter is discovered, a teenager or aged parent causes trouble, or an angry fight occurs.

Frequently, the counselee exaggerates the situation and concludes that all of his or her work is for nothing. The counselor needs to help the counselee remember that the goal is a reconstructed, stronger marriage. The counselor should rehearse how to accomplish the goal and encourage the person to keep focused in positive directions that will achieve the goal.

Marriage Doesn't Mean Happiness

An unhappy person before marriage is likely to be an unhappy person after marriage. Marriage may provide a temporary change in happiness because of the novelty of the situation, but eventually each mate will settle back into the level of happiness experienced as a single adult.

Married life, after all, is not exclusively made up of picnics, dinners out, roses, and little surprise gifts. It is ordinary living, with not enough money, too much work, and too much stress in an uptight world. It is good mixed with bad. If a couple believes marriage is going to be just like courtship, they will be continually frustrated. They will blame themselves or each other for what appears to be a failed marriage. But it's not a failed marriage—it's just life.

Unfortunately, some people keep jumping from one marriage partner to another, ignoring the stark reality that marriage can only be as satisfying as the sum of its participants. Putting two unhappy people together ultimately means there is *double* the *un*happiness.

No Hope of Improving the Other One

Before marriage each one subconsciously said, "Well, he (or she) isn't exactly what I want, but I'll be able to make all the necessary improvements." And there will be *some* improvements. People do modify and adapt, but usually only in areas that are inconsequential.

When we were first married, Sally wanted me to be neater—to throw my dirty laundry in the laundry basket, etc.—and I wanted her to tolerate a little more messiness.

Another early difference was that after a hard Sunday morning of preaching and teaching, I wanted to leave the Sunday dishes and take a nap, turn off the world, hold each other, fall asleep together, or make love. But Sally would say, "I can't relax when I know there's a pile of dirty dishes in the kitchen."

These sound like some of the more easily solved problems of married life, don't they? We *have* adapted to each other. Both of us have made compromises. (We eventually got a dishwasher, so now we can go to bed. This arrangement is a lot more fun!) But after more than thirty-eight years of being married to each other, those conflicting traits continue to come up. Sally is basically tidy. I am basically messy. Recently I asked, "How do you handle my messiness?"

She said, "I learned early to just throw your socks in the laundry basket, close the closet door, and forget them."

After a few years of marriage, people either accept the fact that their mate is different or the very differences will eat holes in the relationship. Differences that once were "cute," can become maddening irritations that drive people apart.

Avoidance Becomes a Pattern

Poor marriages seem to be marked by avoidance. Both partners use ingenious devices to keep from communicating with the other about who they really are and the needs they have. Favorite avoidance tricks are: time away at the job, raising children, church or community activities, being a "couch potato" in front of the TV, or working extra hours or jobs to pay off a mortgage, buy a second car, a boat, or a cottage at the lake.

Eda LeShan tells of a woman who discovered that her husband was having an affair. "He was finally forced into admitting some of the negative feeling he had had about their relationship all along: the times he felt he was being manipulated; the times he became utterly weary of her histrionics; the times he had felt imprisoned by her dependency and proprietary attitude. [The wife] said, 'He kept telling me that he hadn't wanted to hurt my feelings—so instead he took the chance of destroying our marriage.'"[21]

Counsel in Partnership with a Support Network

In typical marriage counseling the counselor and one person meet periodically and concentrate on the problems or issues that are presented in the session by the counselee. We suggest that the counselor be more *proactive* by encouraging:

1. Standard counseling sessions.

2. Specific homework (books to read, tapes to listen to, Scripture assignments, new actions to practice).

3. Involvement in a support group.

4. Help with legal and financial concerns from competent laypeople within the church or community.

People who have a broad-based support network are more likely to continue working on their marriage than those who have a counselor-only support base. Also, a great deal of power and psychological change are accomplished by encouraging personal spiritual development in the individual and enlisting a prayer support group for the situation.

Think of the person with a marriage crisis in the same way you think of the alcoholic who needs frequent support and cannot wait for a counseling appointment. The counselee needs support from peers who have struggled through and survived problem marriages.

The counselor should continue to play an important role but should not try to be the primary support. The counselor is strategic in overseeing a synergistic process that includes counseling sessions, homework, group interaction, and outside legal and financial coaching.

Counsel with God Present

When I start a counseling session, my first question to the counselee generally is, "Well, what can I do for you?" While the person is telling his or her story and moving deeper toward the real problems, part of me is listening and part of me is praying, "Dear God, help me! Give me the insights I need. Give this person the courage to change. Work in the circumstances of his or her life. Help him or her to find the needed support group. Bring about growth and change so that the marriage can be saved."

When I was working on a graduate degree in counseling, I thought I was learning all of the answers, procedures, and techniques I would need to help people get better. My last course was a seminar where I was the only student. I had two professors—one psychologist and one psychiatrist. The sessions consisted of listening to excerpts from recorded counseling sessions I had held with people in my church and community. Then we would discuss the individual's problems and the procedures that ought to be taken.

On one occasion, I presented a tape from my first session with a particular woman. After listening to it I asked my two professors, "Well, what direction should I take with this woman?" They both looked at me blankly, and said, "We don't know."

I had imagined that these men were the fountains of all knowledge about the human psyche and that I would be able to absorb all of their insights and put them to work immediately. I was shocked by how little absolute knowledge they had.

On my way home I came to a deep spiritual awareness that

ultimately only God knew the heart and circumstance of any of my counselees. Unless I enlisted him in the healing process, I would never see the full healing that I wanted for people.

I'm glad for all the training I've had and you've had. The more, the better. But remember to carry out all of your counseling with a deep sense that God understands your people better than you do. And he wants to see them fully healed and restored.

I've also found that God can work inside people day after day, twenty-four hours a day, even when they are not in a counseling session or doing prescribed homework. I urge you to let God be the vital power that he wants to be in your people's lives.

Marriage restoration is a big job—but a "do-able one!" Many of the marriages that are breaking apart could be saved with proper *prevention* and *intervention!*

The Bible says, "He who finds a wife finds what is good" (Proverbs 18:22). We add, "Whoever restores a marriage is replacing generations of pain with health and happiness."

Keep on helping the people who have found a good thing—marriage—and help them keep it good.

Jim and Sally Conway
Fullerton, CA
1992

Notes

Chapter 1—Don't Panic

1. *The Orange County Register*, Santa Ana, CA, October 7, 1991.

Chapter 2—Have Hope

1. Romans 5:5.

2. 1 Corinthians 10:13; James 1:12–16; Jude 24–25. We can claim the *resurrection triumph of Jesus* to win over Satan's plots to destroy our marriage. Christ has defeated the devil for us, and we can appropriate that victory for our own (1 Corinthians 15:57–58; Romans 8:1). We can pray for God to give us wisdom in everything we say, every action we take, and every thought we have (James 1:5; John 16:13; Romans 8:26–28). We can ask for his peace and protection (Psalm 4:8; John 14:26–27; 1 Corinthians 15:58; 2 Corinthians 1:3–5). He will give us the courage to make the needed changes in ourselves.

3. Ed Wheat, M.D., *How to Save Your Marriage Alone*, (Grand Rapids, MI: Zondervan, 1983), 13.

Chapter 5—Vow to Work Hard

1. James 1:5; John 16:13.

2. Philippians 4:13,19.

3. Psalm 103:3–18; 1 Peter 5:7–11.

4. Galatians 6:1–3.

Chapter 6—Handle Your Mate's Affair Wisely

1. J. Allan Petersen, *The Myth of the Greener Grass*, (Wheaton, IL: Tyndale, 1983; rev. 1991), 29.

2. Petersen, 27.

3. Proverbs 2:16; 22:14; Mark 7:21–23; Romans 1:26–29; 1 Corinthians 6:9–10; Ephesians 5:5; Colossians 3:5–6; 1 Thessalonians 4:3–4; 1 Timothy 1:10–11; Hebrews 13:4.

4. 1 Corinthians 10:13.

5. 1 Peter 5:7.

6. Dr. Ed Wheat, *How to Save Your Marriage Alone*, (Wheaton, IL: Tyndale, 1983), 29–30.

7. Wheat, 31–32.

Chapter 7—Walk in Your Spouse's Shoes

1. Adapted from Jim Conway, *Making Real Friends in a Phony World*, (Grand Rapids, MI: Zondervan, 1991), 131.

Chapter 9—Deal with Emotional Clutter

1. Jim Conway, *Adult Children of Legal or Emotional Divorce*, (Downers Grove, IL: InterVarsity, 1990).

2. Beth E. Brown, *When You're Mom No. 2*, (Ann Arbor, MI: Servant, 1991).

Chapter 10—Consider the Career Pressure

1. From the research of Jim and Sally Conway as published in *Adult Children of Legal or Emotional Divorce* by Jim Conway, (Downers Grove, IL: InterVarsity, 1990).

2. Richard Bolles, *What Color Is Your Parachute?*, (San Francisco: Ten Speed Press, 1970, revised annually).

Chapter 11—Build Your Mate's Self-Esteem

1. 1 Corinthians 15:10.

Chapter 14—Flex, Change, and Grow

1. Sally Conway, *Your Husband's Mid-Life Crisis*, (Elgin, IL: David C. Cook, 1980, rev. 1987).

Chapter 15—Know Your Boundaries

1. Ronald Potter-Efron and Patricia Potter-Efron, *I Deserve Respect*, (Center City, MN: Hazeldon Educational Materials, 1989). This helpful booklet is available from Hazeldon, P.O. Box 176, Center City, MN 55012-0176. Telephone: 1-800-328-9000.

Chapter 17—Put Yourself in God's Hand

1. Psalm 40:1–4; Romans 7:14–25.

2. Romans 3:10–12; Isaiah 53:6; Romans 3:23.

3. Romans 5:8; 1 Corinthians 15:3–4; Ephesians 1:7.

4. John 3:16.

5. For example, see Matthew 7:9–11 and Psalm 103:13.

6. Romans 8:31–39.

7. John 10:27–30.

8. Psalm 5:12.

9. Psalm 61:3–4.

10. Psalm 61:4; Matthew 23:37.

11. Psalm 118:7.

12. Romans 8:31.

13. Psalm 138:8.

Chapter 18—Rebuild Carefully

1. Matthew 7:24–27.

2. From the chapter, "Forgiving the Past" by Jim Conway, *Adult Children of Legal or Emotional Divorce*, (Downers Grove, IL: InterVarsity, 1990), 205–220.

3. *Adult Children of Legal or Emotional Divorce*, 216.

4. Jim and Sally Conway, *Traits of a Lasting Marriage*, (Downers Grove, IL: InterVarsity, 1991).

5. For example, see H. Grunebaum, "Middle Age and Marriage: Affiliative Men and Assertive Women," *American Journal of Family*, Fall 1979, Vol. 7, No. 3, 46–50.

Chapter 19—Encourage Hurts to Heal

1. Lewis Smedes, *Forgive & Forget: Healing the Hurts We Don't Deserve*, (San Francisco: Harper & Row, 1984; New York: Pocket Books, div. of Simon and Schuster, 1986), pp. 125–157.

2. *Forgive & Forget*, 138.

3. David Seamands, *Healing for Damaged Emotions*, (Wheaton, IL: Victor, 1981), 128.

4. J. Allan Petersen, *The Myth of the Greener Grass*, (Wheaton, IL: Tyndale, 1983; rev. 1991), 139.

Chapter 20—Invest for a Lifetime

1. Matthew 25:14–30.

Chapter 21—Work for Restoration, Not Divorce

1. U.S. National Center for Health Statistics, *Monthly Vital Statistics Report*, Vol. 31, No. 12 (March 14, 1983).

2. Jim and Sally Conway, *Traits of a Lasting Marriage* (Downers Grove, IL: InterVarsity, 1991).

3. Hugh Carter and Paul C. Glick, *Marriage and Divorce: A Social and Economic Study*, rev. ed. (Cambridge, MA.: Harvard University, 1976).

Arthur J. Norton, "Family Life Cycle: 1980," *Journal of Marriage and the Family*, Vol. 45, No. 2 (May 1983), 267–275.

4. Edward Thorndike, *Adult Learning* (New York: Macmillan, 1928).

5. Charlotte B. Buhler (Malchowski), Edeltrud Baar, Lotte Danzinger-Schenk, Gertrud Falk, and others, *The Child and His Family*, Henry Beaument, trans., (New York: Harper, 1939).

6. Erik Erikson, *Childhood and Society* (New York: Norton, 1950).

7. Robert Havighurst and Ruth Albrecht, *Older People* (New York: McKay, 1953).

8. Bernice Neugarten, ed., *Personality in Middle and Late Life* (New York: Atherton, 1964).

9. Alan B. Knox, *Adult Development and Learning* (San Francisco: Jossey-Bass, 1977).

10. Daniel J. Levinson, *Seasons of a Man's Life* (New York: Alfred A. Knopf, 1978).

11. Roger Gould, *Transformations* (New York: Simon and Schuster, 1978).

12. Marjorie Lowenthal, Majda Thurner, and David Chiriboga, *Four Stages of Life* (San Franscisco: Jossey-Bass, 1975), 49–50.

13. William J. Lederer and Don D. Jackson, M.D., *The Mirages of Marriage* (New York: Norton, 1968), 27.

14. Floyd and Harriett Thatcher, *Long-Term Marriage* (Waco, TX: Word, 1980), 21.

15. Jim Conway, *Adult Children of Legal or Emotional Divorce* (Downers Grove, IL: InterVarsity, 1990).

16. Some of this material is taken from *Traits of a Lasting Marriage* by Jim and Sally Conway (Downers Grove, IL: InterVarsity, 1991).

17. James A. Peterson, *Married Love in the Middle Years* (New York: Association Press, 1968), 20.

18. Thatcher, 20.

19. Richard L. Strauss, *Marriage is for Love* (Wheaton, IL: Tyndale House Publishers, Inc., 1973), 9–10.

20. Jim Conway, *Men in Mid-Life Crisis* (Elgin, IL: David C. Cook, 1978).
Sally Conway, *Your Husband's Mid-Life Crisis* (Elgin, IL: David C. Cook,

1980, rev. 1987).

Jim & Sally Conway, *Women in Mid-Life Crisis* (Wheaton, IL: Tyndale, 1983).

Jim & Sally Conway, *Your Marriage Can Survive Mid-Life Crisis* (Nashville, TN: Nelson, 1987).

21. Eda J. LeShan, *The Wonderful Crisis of Middle Age* (New York: David McKay, 1973), 161.

Recommended Reading

Stephen Arterburn and David Stoop, *When Someone You Love Is Someone You Hate*, Word, 1988.

David Augsburger, *Caring Enough to Forgive/Not Forgive*, Regal, 1981.

Richard Bolles, *What Color Is Your Parachute?* Ten Speed, 1970, revised annually.

Beth E. Brown, *When You're Mom No. 2*, Servant, 1991.

Rich Buhler, *New Choices, New Boundaries*, Nelson, 1991.

Andre Bustanoby, *When Your Mate Is Not a Christian*, Zondervan, 1989.

Gary Chapman, *Hope for the Separated*, Moody, 1982.

Gary Collins, *You Can Make a Difference*, Zondervan, 1992.

Jim Conway, *Making Real Friends in a Phony World*, Zondervan, 1991.

Jim Conway, *Adult Children of Legal or Emotional Divorce*, InterVarsity, 1990.

Jim Conway, *Men in Mid-Life Crisis*, David C. Cook, 1978.

Sally Conway, *Your Husband's Mid-Life Crisis*, David C. Cook, 1980, rev. 1987.

Sally Conway, *Menopause: Help and Hope for This Passage*, Zondervan, 1990.

Jim and Sally Conway, *Women in Mid-Life Crisis*, Tyndale, 1983.

Jim and Sally Conway, *Maximize Your Mid-Life*, Tyndale, 1987.

Jim and Sally Conway, *Your Marriage Can Survive Mid-Life Crisis*, Nelson, 1987.

Jim and Sally Conway, *Traits of a Lasting Marriage*, InterVarsity, 1991.

Becki Conway Sanders, and Jim and Sally Conway, *Trusting God in a Family Crisis*, InterVarsity, 1992.

James Dobson, *What Wives Wish Their Husbands Knew About Women*, Tyndale, 1975.

Don and Jan Frank, *When Victims Marry Victims*, Here's Life, 1990.

Archibald Hart, *Healing Life's Hidden Addictions*, Servant, 1990.

Earl Henslin, *The Way Out of the Wilderness*, Nelson, 1991.

Gordon MacDonald, *Rebuilding Your Broken World*, Nelson, 1988.

Gavin and Patti MacLeod, *Back on Course*, Revell, 1987.

Josh McDowell, *Building Your Self-Image*, Tyndale, 1984.

J. Allan Petersen, *The Myth of the Greener Grass*, Tyndale, 1983; rev. 1991.

Dennis and Barbara Rainey, *Building Your Mate's Self-Esteem*, Here's Life, 1986.

Larry Richards, *When It Hurts Too Much to Wait*, Word, 1985.

David Seamands, *Healing for Damaged Emotions*, Victor, 1981.

David Seamands, *Healing of Memories*, Victor, 1985.

Jan Silvious, *Please Don't Say You Need Me*, Zondervan, 1989.

Gary Smalley and John Trent, *The Blessing*, Word, 1986.

Lewis Smedes, *Forgive & Forget: Healing the Hurts We Don't Deserve*, Harper and Row, 1984; Pocket Books, 1986.

Charles Swindoll, *Strike the Original Match*, Multnomah, 1980.

Jim Talley, *Reconcilable Differences*, Nelson, 1991.

Floyd and Harriett Thatcher, *Long-Term Marriage*, Word, 1980.

Ed Wheat, M.D., *How to Save Your Marriage Alone*, Zondervan, 1983.

Ed Wheat, M.D., *Intended for Pleasure*, Revell, 1977.

Ed and Gaye Wheat, *Love Life for Every Married Couple*, Zondervan, 1980.

Sandra Wilson, *Release from Shame*, InterVarsity, 1990.

H. Norman Wright, *Communication: Key to Your Marriage*, Regal, 1979.

Sally Christon Conway, M.S., and Jim Conway, Ph.D.

Jim and Sally are cofounders of **Mid-Life Dimensions/Christian Living Resources, Inc.**, a California-based organization that offers help to people struggling to save or rebuild their marriages.

Jim and Sally speak together at colleges, seminaries, churches, and retreat centers. They also make television appearances and can be heard on many radio programs. Besides their own books, which are listed in the Recommended Reading section, they have contributed to many other books and magazines. They previously were speakers on their own national daily radio program, **Mid-Life Dimensions**, broadcast on more than two hundred stations.

Jim served as a pastor for almost thirty years, while Sally served as pastor's wife. Sally also has been an elementary school remedial reading specialist. For five years Jim directed the Doctor of Ministry program at Talbot School of Theology, Biola University, and was associate professor of practical theology. Sally taught part-time at Talbot for five years.

Sally holds a Bachelor of Science degree in elementary education and a Master of Science degree in human development. Jim holds two master's degrees—one in psychology and one in theology—and two doctorates—a D.Min. in ministry and a Ph.D. in adult development and learning.

Jim and Sally have three daughters, three sons-in-law, three grandsons, and three granddaughters.

To contact Jim and Sally, write to them in care of Zondervan Publishing House, 5300 Patterson, S.E., Grand Rapids, MI 49530.